The Sultan's Seraglio

Ottaviano Bon

THE SULTAN'S SERAGLIO
An Intimate Portrait of Life at the Ottoman Court

(From the Seventeenth-Century Edition of John Withers)

Introduced and annotated by
Godfrey Goodwin

Saqi Books

British Library Cataloguing-in-Publication Data
A catalogue record for this book is available from the
British Library

ISBN 0 86356 215 9 (hb)
ISBN 0 86356 046 6 (pbk)

In-house editor: Jana Gough

Typeset in Venetian 12 pt

This edition first published 1996
Saqi Books
26 Westbourne Grove
London W2 5RH

To Gillian

Acknowledgements

This book has necessitated the pursuit of Ottaviano Bon, Sir Paul Pindar and John Greaves and I am indebted to my wife and David Castillejo for their expert advice. None of us, alas, has found out anything about Robert Withers, who is the villain of the story—the search has been diligent but each trail has proved false. I have always to thank André Gaspard and Jana Gough for their support and have pleasure in thanking them again. When David Castillejo asked how a confidential report by the Venetian ambassador managed to appear in English under a different name I did not foresee the travel which would ensue in both time and place: still less the support of which I would be in need.

Contents

Contents

V.

Of the Agiamoglans, *how taken, distributed, and imployed.*

VI.

Of the King's Itchoglans, *their severe discipline, and education
in four Subordinate Schools; and of their after advancements.*

VII.

Of inferior persons, as Buffons, Mutes, Musicians;
of the white Eunuchs, *and of the Grand Officers of the* Seraglio.

VIII.

Of the Black Eunuchs, *and* Blackmoor *girls, and women;
of the Physicians, and of the King's children.*

IX.

*Of the cooks, kitchens; diet of the King, Queen, and others;
of the manner of Service; of their skullery, and provision of the* Seraglio.

X.

*Of apparel, bedding, sickness, hospitals, inheritance, King's expences,
recreations, his going abroad, receiving of petitions; of the King's stables, and*
Byram *solemnities.*

XI.

Of the Old Seraglio, *and womens lives therein: of their marriages,
and children: slave-selling, and witnesses.*

XII.

*Of their religion, opinions, Clergymen, times, places, and rites sacred;
and of the womens small devotion.*

A Note on Spelling

The splendid and idiosyncratic spelling of the period has not been touched unless it is clearly due to a careless printing error. However, the use of *f* as one form of *s* has been abandoned for the sake of clarity. Some spellings of Turkish names can only be called flamboyant but are remarkably effective transliterations of the sound of the language. These spellings have been left unchanged.

Withers' additions to Bon's text are set in square brackets, while curly brackets indicate parts of Bon's account omitted by Withers but restored in the present edition.

A glossary records variations in Withers' spelling, the modern Turkish form and an English translation or equivalent.

Introduction

by
Godfrey Goodwin

Tourists flow into the palace of Topkapı in Istanbul, a place which is as romantic as if built in the Baghdad of Haroun al-Rashid. But the viziers and eunuchs, soldiers and fabulously beautiful women who surrounded the sultan, the Shadow of God on Earth, are long gone. Now the corridors are empty, the most secret chambers unscented and the warders and guides lay no claim to be the most beautiful girls in the world.

It was not so before the end of the nineteenth century. Then only the imagination could penetrate the harem or recline in the Pearl Kiosk above the Sea of Marmara, or smoke a hookah in the bedchamber of the Valide Sultan (the royal mother of the sultan), who long before had been bought as a slave. Some contemporary accounts of life inside the Saray (palace) were serious attempts to weigh the evidence or were even based on conversations with Ottoman officials, as was the case with Ottaviano Bon. A great many more were written by gossips dressed up as spies. Of others we know little more than their bottoms as they peer through keyholes like so many hopeful Edwardian holiday-makers in an amusement arcade, squinting into those telescopes of sin which for a penny showed the eager youth what the butler saw. Which was not very much.

Bon's account is very different. Because it was based on as accurate information as he could obtain, it is of lasting interest. A problem arises, however. There was an original version of the manuscript published in

1625 and a new version with additions in 1650. It is with the exploration of the reasons for this that the present Introduction is concerned.

The Sultan

Sultan Ahmet I was born on 18 April 1590 and was only 13½ years old when his father, Mehmet III, died on 21 December 1603. His mother was a woman of strong personality and probably of Greek origin like so many of the Valide Sultans, or Queen Mothers. They had to be tough in order to control a potentially turbulent harem fraught with emotional conflicts because the lives of sons were at stake in the fight for the throne.

Thus it is possible that it was Ahmet's mother, Handan Valide, who ended the Ottoman law of fratricide that had been introduced in the fifteenth century by Fatih ('the Conqueror') Mehmet II in order to avoid a struggle for the accession on a sultan's death. If she had prevented Ahmet from ordering the execution of his younger brother (who was also her younger son, briefly to reign as the degenerate Sultan Mustafa I), then this would have been a powerful reason for Ahmet's dislike of his mother. It is significant that although she was automatically appointed regent on his accession, she was executed on 26 November 1605. It has been claimed that her death was due to harem intrigue although it is not clear who, in effect, became the acting Valide. Moreover, there could have been political reasons.

The fact that Ahmet was so young in 1604, and that he had barely taken hold of his rights as sovereign when Ottaviano Bon left Istanbul in 1607, explains why the Venetian ambassador's account only deals with the sultan in the abstract. He writes of the imperial duties rather than of a boy who exercised them. The idea that a teenager approved legal decisions or senior appointments is absurd. The empire was better governed than such a situation would imply.

The Venetian Envoy

Ottaviano Bon was sent to Istanbul as Bailo, or Venetian representative both of the Senate and of Venetian subjects resident in the city. On the accession of a new sultan it was important that a senior diplomat should appraise any likely future changes in policy, especially towards Venice and its trade. Bon was to stay for some two and a half years, leaving in 1607.

The new Bailo came of a distinguished family. His father Alessandro was Procurator of State when the boy was born in 1551. Ottaviano was educated at the University of Padua under the much admired philosopher, Francesco Piccolomini. A clever student, Bon pursued an equally successful career in provincial government where his diligence and integrity were applauded.

His reputation and his acquaintance with the leaders of the Venetian government made him an obvious choice as Ambassador Extraordinary to the Court of Spain in order to negotiate a treaty which was as important as it was complex, if only because of the economic clauses related to trade. He reached Valladolid on 10 September 1601 and two days later was presented to the king and queen by the resident Venetian envoy. The negotiations dragged on until 1602, when Bon returned to Venice to report to the Senate on Christmas Eve, 24 December.

His posting to Istanbul was equally difficult and even more important to Venetian trade. His embassy was accounted a success and his powers of diplomacy were to be used again after his return home. Two days after an operation to remove a gallstone, he died on 18 December 1622.

A Venetian Bailo was expected to send a fortnightly report to his government but no dispatches from Bon to Venice have yet been discovered: clearly, they would be a vital political record if found. What do survive are the reports written on the completion of his mission. Of all the accounts by Western diplomats and travellers between 1453 (when Constantinople fell to Mehmet II) and the end of the seventeenth century, Bon's is the most reliable in every respect. He did not visit the harem—nor did any male other than the eunuchs—but he did visit private areas of the Saray where no foreigner and only the highest-ranking officers at the sultan's court had ever penetrated. Only Thomas Dallam's sixteenth-century account[1] is of equal authority, but the area that he visited was limited. It took him on foot across the Fourth Court, where no foreigner had penetrated before, and then to the Pearl Kiosk, where he installed his famous organ (see page 18).

More important than Bon's glimpses of private apartments (when he took advantage of the sultan's absence on campaign or at his palace at

Edirne) were his pains in making friends with senior officials—and clearly he had a gift for making friends—and members of the *ulema* (judiciary). It was from these authoritative sources that he learned the revelatory details which make up the present book. Unlike all too many others, he did not waste time on bribing spies or gossiping at the kitchen door. But it must be remembered that it is his integrity that enhances his own authority: most of what he records is confirmed from other sources but some cannot be verified. There was no need for sensationalism and in this book there is none. Bon only once records women being thrown into the Bosphorus. There is no mention of their standing up and frightening divers. They were dispatched, instead, to the Old Saray along with other retired ladies, most of whom had never seen a sultan.

The Two English Versions

Sir Paul Pindar

The mysterious seventeenth-century publications of the text in English involve at least three people: the English ambassador to Istanbul, Sir Paul Pindar; a youth, Robert Withers; and the Professor of Astronomy at Oxford University, John Greaves. Let us turn first to Sir Paul Pindar, the extraordinary merchant who was ambassador to the Ottoman sultan from 1611 to 1620. As a youth, Pindar believed that he had a gift for trade. He persuaded his father to apprentice him to an Italian merchant established in London and he was rapidly appointed his agent in Venice for some fifteen years. However, it is clear that his mercantile contact with that city extended into the seventeenth century. He it was who acted as agent for the Chancellor, William Cecil, when he decided to protect his money against any possible crisis on the approaching death of Queen Elizabeth. This was in 1602 and occasioned a flying visit to Hatfield House: Pindar had a reputation for being the swiftest of travellers.

Indeed, he appears to have held at least three posts concurrently before becoming an ambassador. Elected consul by the merchants in Aleppo, he continued amassing a phenomenal fortune in Venice while serving the then ambassador in Istanbul, Sir Henry Lello, as his secretary from 1597 to 1607. The dates are significant for our story. Eventually he was to be one of the richest men in England although he lost some of this wealth because of his generous loans to the House of Stuart. His London house[2] was regarded as a wonder, clearly with good reason, but was only to survive in a dilapidated condition into the early nineteenth century. Pindar died on 22 August 1650 and was buried in St Botolph's Church, Bishopsgate, which was a few doors away from his home and of which he was a generous benefactor.

It would seem probable that Pindar knew Bon since they were in Istanbul at the same time and were both lively minds confined to the restricted social round of the diminutive diplomatic corps of the day. If the two did not in fact meet, Pindar had plenty of influential Venetian friends who might have helped him to obtain a copy of Bon's report.

A Young Man on the Make

When Pindar himself became ambassador, a certain Robert Withers either came with him or was already living in Istanbul. He must have been very young since all that we know about him is that he was educated under the protection of the ambassador. This, at least, is almost certainly true but one must suspect his claim to have been taught Turkish by Turkish schoolmasters. Such men worked within the religious system and were very unlikely to instruct a foreigner. If Withers did learn Turkish—and there was no reason why he should not have done—it would have been from a Greek or a member of one of the other minorities. But the vaunt may have seemed important to Withers in order to sustain the impersonation that was to follow.

For Withers claims that Pindar obtained permission for him to visit the Saray—a permission that the ambassador appears to have been unable to obtain for himself—not once, but several times and over many years. Turkish would have been essential in such circumstances. Withers even rashly claims to have visited the holy of holies, the harem. Bon was at pains to point out that he himself could not go there and, with one later exception, no foreigner did so until Slade[3] in September 1829 went with Admiral Sir Pulteney Malcolm—but they never entered the private apartments nor saw an odalisque. No foreigner could do so and hope to retain his head upon his shoulders.

The Scholar Deceived

If a suspect's credentials seem puzzling, it helps if he tells a flat lie. When the Oxford professor, Dr John Greaves, unsuspectingly attributed the book to Withers, one wonders how so remarkable a scholar did not pause to reflect on Withers' continual use of Italianisms when plain English would do perfectly well.

These labours (for which Withers was thanked) had already been published in London in 1625 in Mr Purchase's *Pilgrims*, Part II, of which Greaves makes no mention. He points out, however, that Withers' work was undertaken at the cost and care of Sir Paul Pindar. This complicates matters still further.

It is hard to believe that Pindar knew nothing of the edition of 1625 for he would surely have recognized it as the work of Bon. It is equally hard to believe, at a time when the rich bought all the books worth reading, that Sir Paul, of all men, would have missed a publication on the Ottomans or that friends did not draw his attention to it. It may be that in his papers there was a copy of a letter of rebuke for Withers: unless his former protégé were already dead.

Penzer[4] states that the 1625 edition is inferior to that of 1650: the changes are principally omissions and additions, some of which are critical of the Ottomans. One wonders if the latter may not have been Greaves' asides or merely those of the reprehensible young Withers. Who was the new member of the cast in this drama?

The Scholar Travels East

John Greaves came to Istanbul in pursuit of Greek and Latin authors in or about 1638. He was successful because a *sipahi* (cavalryman) stole the *Almaghest* of Ptolemy from the Saray library for him. This theft was not regarded as dishonourable at the time, but rather an act of rescue (an attitude that continued into the nineteenth century, when miniatures were surreptitiously cut out of albums in order to enrich renowned collections). In Egypt, Greaves was to procure or purchase important Greek, Persian and Arabic manuscripts which he duly and punctiliously catalogued. Before leaving Istanbul, he was given a copy of Withers' translation of Bon's report without knowing that Withers was not the author and that it had already been published in 1625.

Greaves was born at Colmore in Hampshire in 1602 and was already studying at Oxford in 1617. Elected a fellow of Merton College in 1624, he became a master of arts and on 22 February 1630, when only 28 years old, he was appointed Professor of Geometry at Gresham College, London. Seven years later, he was to make a mature Grand Tour which took him to Rome. Armed with a brass foot-ruler divided into 2,000 parts, he was able to study Roman instruments depicted on tombs and establish that the Roman foot was 1,994/2,000 of a British foot.[5] (In Athens, his measurement of the Parthenon established the Roman foot as 24/25 of the Greek.) After this, he proceeded to Istanbul and then to Egypt. This time he carried a 10-foot masonry rod subdivided into 10,000 parts in the hope of establishing the dimensions of the Egyptian cubit from studying the Great Pyramid.[6] He sailed for Leghorn (Livorno) in 1639 with boxes of books, manuscripts and his own notes. In 1643 he returned to Oxford as Savilian Professor of Astronomy and Superior Reader of Linacre's Lecture in Merton College.

On 30 October 1648 the parliamentary visitors ejected him from the university not only because he was a royalist but also because he was accused of appointing only royalists to any post under his control. He had rashly sacked Sir Nathaniel Brent from his wardenship simply because he adhered to the Parliamentary party. Instead he had appointed William Harvey, the illustrious discoverer of the circulation of the blood. Greaves' chests were broken into and his papers and manuscripts were pillaged by soldiers and some lost, although more than half appear to have been surreptitiously recovered by a friend.

Greaves retired to the country and hard work; among the enormous number of books that he completed and published was *The Description of the Grand Seignor's Seraglio* which he dedicated to his cousin, George Tooke. (Tooke was a soldier who wrote books on military matters but is now best remembered as a poet.) Greaves' scientific publications were diverse and included two published posthumously—*Of the Manner of Hatching Eggs at Cairo* and a work on Archimedes. Another of his manuscripts which was not published included an account of the longitude and latitude of Constantinople and Rhodes. He died in 1652.

Withers' Additions

Withers added over 60 lines to Bon's text in the edition of 1625 and yet another 250 lines appear in the 1650 version. These add 10 per cent to the length of the book. Whatever Penzer may have thought, these additions have nothing to do with Bon but a great deal to do with the young translator's somewhat abrasive humour.

The style of these additions is very much that of Withers so that it is difficult to believe that any of the additions were due to Greaves. That Withers may have enlarged the text with his comments after 1625 cannot be proved but if, as it would appear, he passed this version round his friends then these afterthoughts make sense. But we have no idea who was the acquaintance who, after Withers' supposed death, gave a copy to Greaves.

The interpolations reveal Withers' love of Turkish food—for this he must be forgiven, but not for omitting several informative lines from Bon. One notes that while Withers claims to have gained entry to the Saray in the 1625 text, this passage is omitted in that of 1650.

Other Accounts

The other accounts of the Saray by contemporaries or earlier commentators are much more limited in scope than Bon's. They include those of Menavino[7] and other escaped pages in the mid-sixteenth century; and also that of Thomas Dallam. As we have seen, he brought the gift of an organ from Queen Elizabeth to Murat III and set it up in the now ruined Pearl Kiosk. Murat was so interested and sat so close to Dallam that the Lancastrian actually brushed against the sultan. He was relieved to receive plaudits and not the executioner's axe. At the beginning of the eighteenth century there was La Motraye,[8] who claimed to have penetrated the empty chambers of the harem in the guise of assistant to the repairer of the royal clocks: this is probably true. Like so many hustled tourists, he had all too little to report.

After Bon, the most important of the reports is that of the Jewish favourite royal physician of the half-Italian Murat III. The doctors of Istanbul, and of the Saray in particular, were frequently Jewish. Domenico Hierosolimitano[9] (whose surname reveals that he was born in Jerusalem) spent ten years in the Saray and saw much of it, yet his information is curiously mixed: but he alone records that the inner treasury of the sultan was stored in the vaults underneath his bedchamber. He also describes how he had to take a girl's pulse with her arm extended through a curtain while that of a princess was wrapped in muslin as he could neither see nor touch royal flesh. Since this was his only contact with the patient, his diagnosis must have been an inspired guess. He was to make his way to Rome from Istanbul and there became a Catholic convert, hence his Christian name of Domenico.

Hierosolimitano refers to that mania for clocks that La Motraye exploited. It is certainly true that such a mania existed. The best evidence of it is the splendid finial of the throne of Ahmet I—it is not generally known that it is the shell of a defunct timepiece. This is something that Bon never saw and so leaves unrecorded. There is much else that the Venetian Bailo did not see: but what he heard, and accurately recorded, was more than admirable. As for Robert Withers, the young man was allegedly dead or at least departed by 1639 and was never to read Greaves' kind tribute to him in the edition of 1650. He has gone without further trace.

TO HIS
Honoured, and truly Noble FRIEND,
George Tooke, Esq;

Sir,

I Durst not have presumed to a Friend of so much
Honour, and Worth, to present this Description
of the *Turkish* EMPEROR'S Court; but that finding
it to be a Piece of that Exactness, as the like is not
extant in any other Language, and the Argument to be
so noble (treating of the greatest Monarchy upon
Earth; whose Magnificence hath much Resemblance
with that of the *Persians*, in the Scriptures), I thought
it would not be unacceptable, if under your Name it
were communicated to the World. In which I assume
nothing to myself, either as author of the Discourse,
or as Polisher of it; but only an humble Desire of
publickly expressing my Obligations to You. It was
freely presented to me at *Constantinople*, and with the
same Freeness I recommend it to the Reader. The
Name of the Author being then unknown, upon
Inquiry I find it since to be the Work of Mr. *Robert
Withers*; who, by the Favour of the *English* Ambassador,
procuring Admittance into the *Seraglio* (a Courtesy
unusual)[1] and, by Continuance many Years in those
Parts, had Time, and Opportunity, to perfect his
Observations. To him therefore are solely due the

Thanks of the Labour: to me it is sufficient that I have faithfully discharged my Trust, in publishing, since the Author's Death, the Fruits of his Travails;[2] and in communicating to the Reader the Pleasure and Satisfaction of perusing a Relation full of Truth and Exactness: Which, in many Particulars, upon Experience he is able to attest, who is,

Sir,
Your most obliged Friend,
And humble Servant,
JOHN GREAVES.

CHAPTER I

A Description of the Place, Partitions, and manifold Conveniences.

THE SITUATION.

*The *Turkish* word is *Sarai*, borrowed from the *Persian* word *Seraw*, which signifieth a house.

†That is, into the *Bosphorus*, which cometh from the mouth of the *Black-Sea* to the point of the *Seraglio*.

THE COMPASS.

THE GATES.

The *Seraglio*,* wherein the *Grand Seignor* resideth with his Court,[1] is wonderfully well situated, being directly in that place where *Byzantium* stood; upon a point of the *Continent*, which looketh towards the mouth† of the *Black-Sea*, and is in form triangular, two sides whereof are compassed with the *Thracian Bosphorus*, and the third joineth to the rest of the city of *Constantinople*. It is inclosed with a very high and strong wall, upon which there are diverse watch-towers, and is, by computation, about three *Italian* miles in compass.

It hath many gates, some of which open towards the sea-side, and the rest into the city; but the chief gate[2] (which indeed is a very stately one) is one of those towards the city; and by it they go in and out daily; the others being kept shut, till such times as the King, or some of the principal officers of the *Seraglio* cause any of them to be opened, [either for their pleasure to sit by the sea-side (where they have a fair prospect, and may behold the ships sailing to and fro) or for any other occasion. Likewise, if any of the other land-gates be opened, it is either when the King sendeth privately, to put some great man to death, or for the execution of some such secret action;] but they are all lock'd fast in the night again.

The aforesaid chief and common gate is in the day time guarded by a {large and magnificent} company of *Capoochees*,[*3] which change their watch by turns, and in the night likewise by others of the same rank; all which *Capoochees* are under the command of a *Capoochee Bashaw*,[†] which *Capoochee Bashaws* (being six in number) are bound, every week one of them, to lie within the *Seraglio*, for the security and safeguard of the same. And without the gate, about ten or twelve paces off, there stands a little house made of boards upon wheels, in which every night a company of *Janizaries* do watch, who, upon any occasion, are ready to awake those within, and to give them notice of whatsoever sudden accident may happen without.

*Porters.

†Head of the Porters, an officer of good credit.

WATCH-HOUSE UPON WHEELS.

In the night also it is well guarded by the {land and} sea-side; for, in the watch-towers which are upon the wall, there {sleep} diverse *Agiamoglan's*,[‡] which are to watch and see that none come near; and, lest any shipping should dare to attempt some mischief, they have ordnance ready charged, and the gunners lying close by them.

‡Of them you shall read more at large hereafter.

In this *Seraglio* there are many stately rooms, suited to the seasons of the year; the greatest part whereof are built upon plain ground; some upon the hills which are there, and some also upon the sea-side, which are called *Kiosks*, that is, rooms of fair prospect, or (as we term them) banqueting houses, into which the King sometimes goes alone, but most commonly with his concubines, for his recreation.

KIOSKS.

Amongst the aforesaid rooms, is the chamber[4] into which the *Grand Seignor* repaireth, when he is to give audience to Ambassadors, or to the *Bashaws*, on the days of *publick Divan*, and to those who being to depart upon any weighty service, or employment, are to take

CHAMBER OF AUDIENCE.

their leaves of him; as also to such who, after the limited time of their government abroad is expired, do return to *Constantinople*, to give account to his Majesty of their carriage in their several places. This room standeth in a little court curiously adorned with many very delicate fountains, and hath within it a *Sofa** spread with very sumptuous carpets of gold, and of crimson velvet embroidered with costly pearls, upon which the *Grand Seignor* sitteth; and about the chamber, [instead of hangings,] the walls are covered with very fine white stones, which, having diverse sorts of leaves and flowers artificially wrought and bak'd upon them, do make a glorious show. There is also a little room adjoining unto it, the whole inside whereof is covered with silver plate hatch'd with gold, and the floor is spread with very rich *Persian* carpets of silk and gold.[5]

There are, belonging to the said rooms and lodgings of the King, very fair gardens, of all sorts of flowers and fruits that are to be found in those parts, with many very pleasant walks, inclosed with high Cypress trees on each side, and marble fountains in such abundance, that almost every walk hath two or three of them; such great delight doth the *Grand Seignor* and all the *Turks* in general take in them. [Nor indeed doth a *Turk*, at any time, shew himself to be so truly pleased and satisfied in his senses, as he doth in the summer time, when he is in a pleasant garden: for he is no sooner come into it (if it be his own, or where he thinks he may be bold, but he puts off his uppermost coat, and lays it aside, and upon that his *Turbant*,[6] then turns up his sleeves, and unbuttoneth himself, turning his breast to the wind, if there be any; if not, he fans himself, or his servant doth it for him. Again, sometimes standing upon a high bank, to take the fresh air, holding his arms abroad (as a *Cormorant* sitting upon a rock doth his wings in sun-shine after

*A place raised from the floor, about a foot, to sit upon.

GARDENS.

CYPRESS WALKS.

THE PLEASURE THAT A TURK TAKES IN A GARDEN.

a storm) courting the weather, and sweet air, calling it his soul, his life, and his delight; ever and anon shewing some notable signs of contentment: nor shall the garden (during his pleasant distraction) be termed other than *Paradise*, with whose flowers he stuffs his bosom, and decketh his *Turbant*, shaking his head at their sweet favours, and sometimes singing a song to some pretty flower, by whose name peradventure his mistress is called; and uttering words of as great joy, as if at that instant she herself were there present. And one bit of meat in the garden shall do him more good (in his opinion) than the best fare that may be elsewhere.]

Besides the aforesaid rooms (which are very many, and serve only for the King's own person) there is the womens lodging, which is in a manner like a nunnery, wherein the Queen, the other *Sultana's,** and all the King's women and slaves do dwell. And it hath within it all the commodity that may be, of beds, chambers, dining-rooms,[7] *Bagno's,*†[8] and all other kinds of building necessary for the use and service of the women, which dwell therein.

There are likewise diverse rooms and lodgings, built a-part from all those aforesaid, which serve both for the principal Officers and those of a mean degree, and also for the basest sort;[9] and are so well furnished, that not any want can be discerned of ought, that may be thought requisite and convenient for them.

Amongst which there are two large buildings, the one the *Hazineh*, or private treasury; and the other the King's wardrobe. These are two very handsome buildings, and secure by reason of the thickness of their walls, and strength of their iron windows. They have each of them an iron door, kept shut continually, and that of the *Hazineh* sealed with the King's seal.

In the said *Seraglio* there are rooms for prayer,

WOMENS LODGING.

*Sultana, Lady, the feminine gender to *Sultan*.

†Baths of hot-houses; it must be pronounced *Banios*.

ROOMS FOR OFFICERS.

THE PRIVY TREASURY AND WARDROBE.

DOOR SEALED.

ROOMS FOR MANY
OTHER USES.

Bagno's, schools,[10] butteries, kitchins, distilling-rooms, places to swim in,[11] places to run horses in, places for wrestling, butts to shoot at,[12] and to conclude, all the commodity that may be had in a Prince's Palace, for things of that nature.

FIRST GATE.

At the first entrance into the *Seraglio*, there is a very large and stately gate,[13] in the porch whereof, there is

PORCH AND GUARD.

always a guard of about fifty men with their weapons by them, as pieces, bows, and swords. Having passed this gate (through which the *Bashaws* and other great

GREAT COURT.

men may pass on horse-back) there is a very spacious court almost a quarter of an *Italian* mile in length, and very nigh as much in breadth; and, on the left hand in the court near unto the gate, there is a place to shelter the people and horses in rainy weather. On the right

HOSPITAL, WITH
OFFICERS.

hand there is an Hospital,[14] for such as fall sick in the *Seraglio*, in which there are all things necessary: it is kept by an Eunuch, who hath many servants under him to attend upon the diseased. Again, on the left

STOREHOUSE.

hand there is a very large place in which they keep their timber, and carts, and such like things, to have them near at hand for the use and service of the *Seraglio*; over which there is a great hall, where are hanged up many weapons of antiquity, as scimitars, javelins, bows, head-pieces, gauntlets, etc.[15] which they keep to lend the soldiers and others, for to accompany

*The *Grand Seignor's*
Deputy.

the *Grand Seignor*, or the *Great Vizir*,* when they make any solemn entry into the city of *Constantinople*.

Having passed through the aforesaid court, there

SECOND GATE.

is a second gate[16] (at which the *Bashaws* alight) somewhat less than the former, but more neat and costly;

PORCH AND GUARD.

under which there is also a stately porch, where there is likewise a guard of *Capoochees* provided with weapons, as they at the first gate are. Thence there is

SECOND COURT.

another court lesser than the former, but far more beautiful and pleasant, by reason of the delicate

*Roe Deer.

(a) Messengers,
Pursuivants, or
Sumners. (b) The
Turkish word is *Yeng-
itcheree*, of *Yenghee* and
Itcheree that is, new
in, for that they are
the latest order of
Soldiers. (c) The
word is *Espawhee*,
which in the *Persian*
signifieth a horse-
man. (d) Court of
Justice.

NINE KITCHINS
WITH THEIR
LARDERS.

†Chief Chamberlain.

‡*Agha* signifieth
Master.

KING'S STABLE.

HORSES
FURNITURE.

fountains, and rows of *Cypress* trees, and the green grass-plots in which the *Gazels** do feed, and bring forth young: but in this court (the *Grand Seignior* only excepted) every one must go on foot. On both sides of the said gate there is an open gallery underset with pillars, without which the (a) *Chiaushes*, the (b) *Janizaries*, and the (c) *Spahees* do use to stand in their several ranks, very well apparelled, at such times as there is a great (d) *Divan* held for the coming of any Ambassador to kiss the *Grand-Signor's* hand.

In the said court on the right hand are all the kitchins, being in number nine; all which have their several officers and larders belonging unto them.

The first and greatest is the King's.[17]

The second the Queen's.[18]

The third the *Sultana's*.

The fourth the *Capee Agha's*.†[19]

The fifth for the *Divan*.

The sixth for the *Agha's*,‡ the King's gentlemen.

The seventh for the meaner sort of servants.

The eighth for the women.

The ninth for the under officers of the *Divan*, and such as attend there to do what belongeth unto them in their several places.

And on the left side of the court there is the King's stable, of about thirty, or thirty five very brave horses, which his Majesty keepeth for his exercise, when he pleaseth to run, or sport with his gentlemen the *Agha's* in the *Seraglio*.[20] Over which stable there is a row of rooms, wherein is kept all the furniture of the horses, the which (I having seen both there, and abroad, at such times as they have been used) I can affirm to be of extraordinary value. For the bridles, pectorals, cruppers, saddle-cloths, the pommels of the saddles, and stirrups, are set so thick with jewels of diverse sorts, that the beholders are amazed, they do so far exceed all imagination.

Near adjoining to the said stable are certain buildings for the service of the officers of the *Divan*, and having passed two thirds of the court on the same side, there is the room wherein the *Divan* is kept: [unto which joineth upon one side the *Hazineh*, called the outward *Hazineh*,] which (the *Divan* being ended) is sealed with the chief *Vizir's Seal*. And even with the room where the *Divan* is kept (but somewhat behind it, towards the left hand) is the gate which leadeth into the womens lodgings, called the Queen's gate, which is kept and guarded by a company of black Eunuchs.

The aforesaid second court endeth at a third gate, termed the King's gate,[21] which leadeth into the rooms and lodgings kept apart for himself, and such gentlemen, as are to attend upon him continually: neither may any one enter therein, but by absolute leave from the King (speaking of men of great quality;) but such as are belonging to the buttery, or kitchin, and physicians, caters, and sewers, may go in and out with leave only from the *Capee Agha*,* who is the chief chamberlain of the *Seraglio*, and to him is committed the keeping of that gate; and he is always at hand (by reason his lodging is near) with a company of white Eunuchs about him like himself; so that what is reported, of things within this gate, is for the most part by relation; for either one may not see them, or if he do see them, it must be when the King is absent; and he must be brought in by some man of quality and command, by one of the gates at the sea-side; the which also cannot be obtained but with great difficulty, and some charge too for a gratification to the guide; they having not only great regard and respect to their King's person, but also to his rooms in his absence.

DIVAN ROOM.

OUTWARD *HAZINEH*, OR TREASURY.

GALLERY, QUEEN'S GATE, AND GUARD OF BLACK EUNUCHS.

THIRD (OR KING'S) GATE.

WHO MAY ENTER.

*Capee Agha chief chamberlain.

WHITE EUNUCHS.

Having passed the third gate (the which hath also a very fair porch) immediately is seen the aforesaid room appointed for publick audience: and there within that gate also is another very fair court, paved with very fine marble, wrought with *Mosaical* work; wherein are many delicate fountains, and sumptuous buildings on all sides, in which commonly the King useth to eat and pass the time in some recreation.

AUDIENCE CHAMBER. ANOTHER FAIR COURT.

It happened, that I taking hold of a fit time, the King being abroad hunting, through the great friendship which was twixt my selfe and the *Kahiyah* of the *Bustangi Bashee*; had the opportunitie (he being my guide) to goe into the *Seraglio*, entring by a gate at the Sea side where he shewed me many of the King's backward roomes, divers *Bagnoes*, and many other curious and delightfull things, both for the excellencie of their gilding, and the abundance of Fountaynes that were in them.[22]

SUMMER ROOMS.

There is a row of summer rooms built upon the top of a little hill; which looks towards the sea-side, so well contrived with halls and chambers, and so pleasantly seated, and richly furnished, that it may well be the habitation of so great a Prince. Amongst which there is a hall opening towards the East, but

A HALL.

underset with very fair pillars; which hall looks into an

A LAKE.

artificial four square lake[23] (which they call *Hawoz*) proceeding from about thirty fountains which are built upon a kind of *Terras*, of very fine marble, which compasseth the said lake, the water running from the fountains above down into the lake, and from the lake through diverse gutters into gardens. Two men may walk abreast upon the *Terras*, where they hear the continual and sweet harmony, which the fountains make with leaden pipes, insomuch that it is a most delightful place. And in the lake there is a little boat,

A LITTLE BOAT IN THE LAKE.

the which (as I was informed) the *Grand Seignor* doth

oftentimes go into with his *Mutes*,* and *Buffoons*, to
make them row up and down, and to sport with them,
making them leap into the water; and many times, as
he walks along with them above upon the sides of the
lake, he throws them down into it, and plunges them
over head and ears.

GRAND SEIGNOR'S
BED-CHAMBER
DESCRIBED.

Near unto the said hall, is his Majesty's bed-
chamber,[24] the walls whereof are covered with stones
of the finest *China* metal, spotted with flowers of
diverse colours, which make an excellent show.[25] The
Anteporta's† are of cloth of gold of *Bursia*,[26] and their

†Hangings before
the doors.

borders of crimson velvet embroidered with gold and
pearls: the posts of the bedstead are of silver, hollow,
and, instead of knops on the tops of them, there are

LIONS OF CHRISTAL.

set lions made of christal: the canopy over it is of
cloth of gold, and so are the bolsters, and the
mattresses. The floor of this chamber (as of the other
rooms) and the *Sofa's*, are spread with very costly
Persian carpets of silk and gold; and the pallets to sit
on, with the cushions to lean upon, are of very rich
{and pure Bursa} cloth of gold.

A LANTERN.

There is hanging, in the midst of the aforesaid hall,
a very great lantern, the form whereof is round, and
the bars of silver gilt, and set very thick with rubies,
emeralds, and *Turquoises*: the panes are of fine christal.

BASEN AND EWER
OF GOLD.

There is likewise a bason and ewer of massy gold, set
with rubies and *Turquoises*, which beautify the room.

SHOOTING PLACE.

Behind the hall, there is a place to shoot in, where
there are laid up many bows and arrows; and there are
to be seen such strange passages made with arrows by
the King's predecessors, and by the King himself,
through brass and iron, that it seemeth almost
impossible to be done by the arm of any man.

PUBLICK *DIVAN*
DESCRIBED.

The room, which is called the *Publick Divan*,[27] hath
been built of late years. It is four square, and about
eight or nine paces every way from side to side. It hath

behind it another room for the service thereof, and one also at the coming in to the *Divan* on the right hand, divided only by a wooden rail: with many other rooms somewhat distant from it, which serve for the expedition of sundry businesses. This *Divan* I call publick, because any kind of person whatsoever (as well stranger as native) publickly and indifferently may have free access unto it, to require justice, to procure grants, and to end their causes, and controversies, of what nature, condition, or import soever they be, without let or contradiction.

Thus have I made a brief description of some of the rooms and buildings of this *Seraglio*, according to the notice I took of them. But hitherto I have omitted to shew, how that a great part of the best of them have been built, from time to time, at the cost and charges of the subjects. For there have been diverse *Bashaws*, who being in favour with the *Grand Seignor* obtained leave at several times to add unto the *Seraglio* a room or two, for a memorial of some notable good service which they had done their Prince. In the building of which, they have spared no cost, although for the most part the rooms are very little: but this their often patching of new rooms with old hath caused a great confusedness in the whole fabrick, they having not observed any uniformity at all in their manner of building.[28]

Of the Divan Days, Judges, Session, Judicature, Diet, and giving an Account to the King of what hath passed.

FOUR *DIVAN* DAYS.

*Chief *Vizir*.

†The true word is *Kazee-asker*, which signifieth, the Judge of an Army.

‡*Defterdars*, the Treasurers: so called of the word *Defter*, which signifieth a bill or Scroul.

§The word signifieth a Keeper of the Mark.

SECRETARIES AND CLERKS.

¶Chief over all the *Chiaushes*.

CHIAUSHES.

The *Divan* days are four every week, *viz.* *Saturday, Sunday, Monday,* and *Tuesday*; upon which days the *Vizir Azem*,*[1] with all the rest of the *Vizirs*, the two *Cadileschers*† of *Grecia*[2] and *Natolia* (which are the chief over all the *Cadees* of those two provinces,) the three *Defterdars*,‡ (whose charge is to gather in the King's revenues, and likewise to pay all his soldiers, and others which have any pension due unto them;) the *Reiskitawb* (which is the chancellor) the *Nishawngee*§ (that is, he that signeth commandments and letters with the *Grand Seignor's* mark) the secretaries of all the *Bashaws*, and of other great men; a great number of clerks, which are always attending at the door of the *Divan*; the *Chiaush Bashaw*¶ (who, all that while that he is in the *Seraglio*, carrieth a silver staff in his hand) and many *Chiaushes*, that, at the *Vizir's* command, they may be ready to be dispatched, with such orders as shall be given them by him, to what place, or to whomsoever he pleaseth, (for they are those which are employed in ambassies, or in ordinary messages, to summon men to appear before the bench, to keep close prisoners, and, in fine, to perform all business of that nature.) Upon those days,

33

I say, all the aforesaid magistrates and officers, from the highest to the lowest, are to be at the *Divan* by break of day.

THE MANNER OF SESSION.

The *Vizirs* being come into the *Divan*, they sit down within, at the further end thereof, with their faces towards the door, upon a low bench, which joineth to the wall, every one in his place, as he is in degree,

LEFT, THE UPPER HAND, WITH THE LAITY, BUT WITH THE CLERGY THE RIGHT.

sitting all at the right hand of the chief *Vizir*, for with the laity the left is counted the upper hand, but with the clergy the right; and, on his left hand, upon the same bench, do sit the two *Cadeleschers*; first, he of

CADELESCHERS PLACES.

Græcia, as being of the more noble and famous province; and then he of *Natolia*. And, on the right side, at the coming in at the door, do sit the three

DEFTERDARS PLACES.

Defterdars, who have behind them (in the aforesaid room, which is divided with a wooden rail) all the said

CLERKS PLACES.

clerks, who sit upon the ground on matts, with paper and pens in their hand, being ready to write whatsoever is commanded them. And, on the other side, over against the *Defterdars*, sits the *Nishawngee*, with

NISHAWNGEE'S PLACE.

a pen in his hand, having his assistants round about him. The *Reiskitawb*, for the most part, stands close by

REISKITAWB'S PLACE.

the *Vizir*, for he takes his advice in many occurrents. In the midst of the room do stand all such as require *audience* of the Bench.

Now they being all come together, and every man set in his own place, the petitioners forthwith begin their suits, one after another, (who have no need of

NO NEED OF ATTORNEYS.

attorneys, though oftentimes they procure the help of a *Chiaush*, for every one may speak for himself) referring themselves to the judgment and sentence of

THE POWER OF THE *VIZIR AZEM*.

the *Vizir Azem*, who (if he please) may end all:[3] for the other *Bashaws* do not speak, but only hearken and attend, till such time as he shall refer any thing to their arbitrement, as he commonly doth. For he having once understood the substance only of a business (to free himself from too much trouble) remits the deciding of it to others; as for example, if it be appertaining to the civil law, he then remits it to the *Cadileschers*; if it be of accounts, to the *Defterdars*; if of falshood (as counterfeiting the mark, or such like) to the *Nishawngee*; if concerning merchants, or merchandize, (wherein there may be any great difficulty) to some one of the other *Bashaws* which sit by him; so that after this manner he doth exceedingly ease himself of so great a toil and burden, which otherwise he alone should be enforced to undergo; reserving only to himself what he thinketh to be of greatest import and consequence; and the like course doth the *Caimekam** take in his absence.

Thus do they spend the time until it be almost noon; at which hour (one of the *Sewers*[4] being appointed to be there present) the chief *Vizir* commands that dinner be brought in; and immediately all the common people depart. So the room being free, the tables are made ready after this manner; there is set upon a stool, before the *Vizir Azem*, a thin round copper plate tinn'd over, about the bigness of the bottom of a beer barrel, at which himself, with one, or two at the most, of the other *Bashaws*, do eat. The like is prepared for the rest of the *Vizers*, which do eat together; and another for the *Cadileschers*; one for the *Defterdars*; and one likewise for the *Nishawngee*. Having every one a napkin[†] spread upon his knees, to keep his garments clean, and, a great quantity of bread being laid ready round the said copper plates, immediately the meat is brought in, and set before them upon the plates, in great dishes made after a strange fashion; and still as they have eaten of one dish, the *Sewer* takes off that, and sets on another. Their diet is ordinarily, mutton, hens, pigeons, geese, lamb, chickens, broth of rice and pulse, dress'd after diverse fashions, and some

MANNER OF DECIDING.

*He which governs in the chief *Vizir's* absence. *Caim* signifieth, firm, or resident, and *Me-Kawm*, a place.

DINNER RITES.

COPPER PLATE.

†Which they call *Eestimawl*.

DIET.

tarts, or such like, at the last; for in a very short space
they make an end of their dinner. That which

remaineth of the said tables, the officers of the *Divan*
do eat; but they have an addition allowed, and brought
them from their kitchin. The *Bashaws*, and other great

men, have drink brought unto them (which is *Sherbet*)
in great *Porcelain* dishes; but the others do either not
drink at all, or, if they do drink, it is fair water
brought them from the next fountains. At the same
time, when the *Vizirs* of the bench, and others of the

Divan, are at dinner, the under officers, waiters, and
keepers, do dine also, (for they must lose no time) the
which is not less ordinarily than four or five hundred
persons (including also such poor sharking fellows as
slip into the company for a dinner) but their food is
nothing but bread and pottage, which they call *Churva*,
which serves to fill their bellies, though it be of small
nourishment.[5]

Dinner being ended, the chief *Vizir* spendeth some
small time about general affairs, and taking counsel
together (if he pleaseth and thinks it fit) with the
other *Bashaws*; at last he determineth and resolveth of
all within himself, and prepareth to go in unto the
King (it being the ordinary custom so to do, in two of
the four *Divan* days, viz. upon *Sunday*, and upon

Tuesday) to render an account briefly unto his Majesty
of all such businesses as he hath dispatched. And, to
this end, the *Grand Seignor* (after he hath dined also)
repaireth unto his chamber of audience, and being set

down upon a *Sofa*, sendeth the *Capee Agha* (who hath in
his hand a silver staff) to call first the *Cadileschers*; who
immediately rise up out of their places, and having
bowed themselves to the *Vizir Azem*, they depart, being
accompanied with the said *Capee Agha* and *Chiaush
Bashaw*, who go before them with their silver staves in
their hands; and so they go in unto the King, to give

account, and make him acquainted with what hath passed concerning their charge; which being done, they are dismissed for that day, and go directly home to their own houses. Next after them are called the

Defterdars; who, in the same manner, are brought unto the King, but the chief *Defterdar* is only permitted to speak; and having dispatched, they take leave, and give

place to the *Vizirs,* who are called last of all, and go together in rank, one after another, the chief *Vizir* being foremost, usher'd along by the two aforesaid

silver staves; and being come before the presence of the *Grand Seignor,* they stand all on one side of the room, with their hands before them across,[6] holding down their heads, in token of reverence and humility. And here none but the chief *Vizir* speaketh, and gives an account of what he thinketh fit, delivering his *Memorials,* or *Arzes,* one by one; the which the King having read, the *Vizir* takes them, and having put them into a little crimson satten bag, he most humbly layeth them down again before his Majesty, who afterwards causeth his *Hattee-humawyoon*[*7] to be drawn

for the performance of what the *Arzes* did require. If the *Grand Seignor* demand no further of him (the other *Bashaws* not having spoken one word all this while) they all depart, and take horse at the second gate; and, being accompanied by divers men of quality (who, to insinuate into their favours, do wait upon them)

besides a great many of their own people, every one goes to his own house. The Chief *Vizir,* for his greater grace and honour, hath commonly about an hundred *Chiaushes* on horseback, who bring him to his home, and so the *Divan* is ended for that day, it being about three[8] hours after noon; but upon such days as they have no audience of the King, they dispatch sooner. And what hath been said of the *Vizir Azem,* the same also is to be understood of the *Caimekam* in his absence.

It is to be noted that sometimes also the *Agha** of the *Janizaries*, and the captain *Bashaw*, come to the *Divan*, when they are at home in *Constantinople*, and have business to do there. But the captain *Bashaw*† only doth go in unto the King (which also may not be but in company of the other *Bashaws*) and his business is to acquaint his Majesty with the estate and affairs of the *Arsenal*, and *Armada*. His place in the *Divan* is upon the same bench, but yet he sitteth last, and lowest, of all the *Bashaws*; unless he be a *Vizir* (as it is often seen) and then he takes his place either second, or third, or fourth, as he is in degree by election. But the *Agha* of the *Janizaries* doth not sit in *Divan*, but sitteth under the open gallery on the right hand within the second gate. And if at any time it shall so fall out, upon some extraordinary business, (as it hath sometimes been seen) that he be to go in unto the King; then he is called first of all, and goeth before either *Defterdars*, or *Cadeleschers*: and being come out again from his Majesty, he sitteth down again in his place until the *Divan* be ended. He is the last that departeth of all the great men, [and is attended on by a great many *Churbegees*†[19] and *Janizaries* unto his *Seraglio*, where he and many of them do live together.]

The *Grand Seignor's* predecessors were always wont to come, and this man sometimes cometh privately by an upper way to a certain little window, which looketh into the *Divan*, right over the head of the Chief *Vizir*; and there sitteth (with a lattise before him, that he may not be seen) to hear and see, what is done in the *Divan*: and especially at such times when he is to give audience to any Ambassador from a great Prince, to see him eat, and hear him discourse with the *Bashaws*: and by this his coming to that window, the Chief *Vizir*

*Chief captain or master of the *Janizaries*.

†Admiral, Captain, *Bashaw*.

HIS PLACE.

AGA OF THE *JANIZARIES* PLACE.

†Captains of the *Janizaries*.

THE KING'S PRIVATE AWFUL WINDOW.

38

(who always standeth in jeopardy of losing his head, upon the *Grand Seignor's* displeasure) is enforced to carry himself very uprightly, and circumspectly, in the managing of affairs, whilst he sits in *Divan*; though at other times his hands are open to bribery, and carry businesses as he pleaseth.

CHAPTER III

Of the Audience and Entertainment given to Ambassadors.

AMBASSADORS
AUDIENCE.

When it falleth out that an Ambassador from any great Prince, is to kiss the *Grand Seignor's* hand; it must be either upon a *Sunday*, or upon a *Tuesday*, (for those are the days appointed for his Highness to give audience) to the end he may not be troubled at other times. And then the *Vizir* commandeth that there be a great *Divan*, which is done by calling together all the *Grandees* of the *Porch*,[1] all the *Chiaushes*, all the *Mutaferrakas*,* and a great number of *Spahees* and *Janizaries*; who are every one of them commanded by their captains, to apparel themselves in the best manner that they are able, and to go every one to his place in the second court, and there to stand in orderly ranks: making indeed a very goodly show, for they are very well clothed, and are most of them of comely personage.

*These are horsemen, but of a higher rank than *Spahees*: the word signifieth set apart, or different.

Thus the *Divan* being all in order, and few, or no common business handled for that day, the *Vizir* sendeth the *Chiaush Bashaw*, with many of his *Chiaushes* on horse-back, to accompany the Ambassador: who, being come to the *Divan*, is set face to face, close before the chief *Vizir*, upon a stool covered with cloth of gold. Having for a while complimented and used

AMBASSADOR
ENTERTAINED AT
THE *DIVAN*.

some friendly discourse together; the *Bashaw* commandeth that dinner be brought: the which is done after the same manner as upon other *Divan* days;

SILVER PLATE. only the round plate, on which the meat is set, is of silver, and the victuals are more delicate and in greater abundance. And so the Ambassador and the *Vizir Azem*, with one or two of the other *Bashaws*, do eat together.

A THOUSAND CROWNS ALLOWED FOR THE ENTERTAINMENT. And for every such banquet at such times, the *Grand Seignor* alloweth, besides the ordinary *Divan* diet, a thousand crowns to be spent. [Howbeit I dare say the steward makes the one half to serve the turn, and reserves the rest to himself.]

They having dined, the *Vizir* entertaineth the Ambassador with some discourse, until such time as the Ambassador's followers have dined also, who I can say are served after a very mean fashion; and then the Ambassador, together with his own attendants, retire themselves into a certain place near the King's gate: where he must stay, till such time as all the orders of the *Divan* have had audience of the King, who being dismissed do all depart, the *Bashaws* excepted, who for the *Grand Seignor's* honour are to stay, and attend in the room upon his Majesty. But by the way I must not omit to tell you, how that the present, which the Ambassador brings along with him, is carried, whilst he sitteth in the said retiring place, once about the second court in open sight of the people, be it what it will, and so in unto the King.

MASTER OF THE CEREMONIES. Then the Ambassador is called by the Master of the ceremonies, by whom he is brought to the gate where the *Capee Agha* standeth with a company of Eunuchs. Then the *Capee Agha* leadeth him to the door of the room, where there do stand two *Capoochee Bashaws*, who

HIS ADMISSION TO THE PRESENCE. HIS KISSING THE KING'S HAND. take the Ambassador, the one by one arm, and the other by the other arm,[2] and so lead him to kiss his Highness's hand, which in truth is but his hanging sleeve;[3] which he having done, they lead him back after the same manner to the lower end of the room, where he standeth till such time as the said two *Capoochee Bashaws* have led such of the Ambassador's gentlemen, as are appointed to kiss the King's hand also. This done, the *Druggaman**[4] declareth the Ambassador's commission, to which the *Grand Seignor* maketh no answer at all, disdaining to speak to a christian; but only speaketh a word or two to the Chief *Vizir*, to license him, referring all proceedings to his discretion. And so the Ambassador departeth, doing obeisance to the King, with bowing down his head, but pulleth not off his hat, or cap at all.[5]

There is one particular, belonging to this ceremony, worthy the observation, which is this; that there is not at any time, any person whatsoever, as well Ambassador as other, which is to kiss the *Grand Seignor's* hand, but he is vested with a vest[6] given him by the *Grand Seignor*. And to this end, before the Ambassador goeth in unto the king, the *Vizir Azem* sendeth him so many vests, as are appointed by *Canon*,[7] for himself and his gentlemen; who put them on in the place where the Ambassador stayeth, till the King send for him to give him audience. These vests are of divers sorts; of which there is one or two for the Ambassador's own person of cloth of gold of *Bursia*; the other being of a low price, worth little or nothing.

But on the contrary, in lieu of those vests, there is not any Ambassador, which is to go to the King for his first audience; or *Bashaw*, who, at his return from some employment aborad, is to kiss his hand, but they present him with the full value of what the *Canon* requireth: insomuch that the *Grand Seignor* receiveth more than he giveth, twenty fold. Moreover, the *Bashaws*, over and above the ordinary duty, do give him exceeding rich presents, and oftentimes great sums of money too; that by all means they may continue in his grace and favour.

Other Ambassadors, which come from petty princes, or states, howbeit they are vested also with vests given them by the *Grand Seignor*, yet they come not to the *Divan* in that pomp, neither are they feasted as the others are; but go privately, carrying their present with them: howsoever, they are also led in unto the King after the aforesaid manner. It is to be noted, that all Ambassadors from absolute Princes, as well ordinary as extraordinary, excepting those from the *Signoria* of *Venice*, to whom, from their first introduction, it was denied: all, I say, lie at the charges of the *Grand Seignor*. For from his own store, they have allowed them wheat, barley, pulse, wood, coals, hay, the custom of their wine, and many other necessaries for their houshold expense; and from the *Defterdar* so many aspars* *per diem*, as the *Vizir* shall think fit. Which provision, tho' now of late it be very hard to be gotten in; yet by great importunity and gifts (without which there is no good to be done) in the end they receive a great part of it. [But the officers will share with them, do what they can; such is their baseness, and slender account, of either honour, or honesty.]

ALL AMBASSADORS BUT THE *VENETIAN* AT THE KING'S CHARGE.

*Ten aspars make six-pence.

Of the Persons which live in the Seraglio; and chiefly of the Women, and Virgins.

ONE LORD, THE
REST SLAVES.

*This word
signifieth an
expeller of Princes:
but some will have
it to come of *Pawd*
and *Shoob*, which is
an expeller of
injury, or injustice;
but amongst the
Turks it is used for
an Emperor; and
they give the same
title to the Emperor
of *Germany*, calling
him *Nemps
Pawdishawh*.

†This is a *Persian*
word, and
signifieth, a man of
blood, or one which
causeth blood; but
used for King.

aving thus far made a description of the
Seraglio itself, and the buildings which are
therein; with some particulars belonging
unto it, according to that which I have both seen, and
heard from others which are daily conversant there: it
followeth that I now speak somewhat touching those
which dwell in it, and of their several qualities and
employments.

First then I say, that all they which are in the
Seraglio, both men and women, are the *Grand Seignor's*
slaves[1] (for so they stile themselves;) and so are all
they which are subject to his empire. For besides that
he is their sovereign, they do all acknowledge that
whatsoever they do possess or enjoy, proceedeth
meerly from his good will and favour: and not only
their estates, but their lives also are at his dispose, not
having respect either to the cause, or manner. [So
that in my opinion, the attributes they give unto him,
are indifferently proper, and fitly suiting with the
condition of such a Prince. For he is stiled sometimes
Pawdishawh,* and sometimes *Hoonkeawr*.† In regard of
sovereignty and justice, they may truly call him *Pawdishawh*; but in regard of his tyranny, *Hoonkeawr*: both

which words they use in the same sense as we do the word King.]

This *Seraglio* may rightly be termed the seminary or nursery of the best subjects. For in it, all they have their education, which afterwards become the principal officers, and subordinate rulers of the state, and affairs of the whole empire; [as hereafter I shall shew at large].

TWO THOUSAND
WITHIN THE KING'S
GATE.

They which are within the third gate, called the King's gate, are about two thousand persons, men and women; whereof the women (old and young one with another; what with the King's concubines, old women, and women servants) may be about eleven or twelve hundred.[2] Now, those which are kept up for their beauties, are all young virgins taken and stolen from foreign nations;[3] who after they have been instructed in good behaviour, and can play upon instruments, sing, dance, and sew curiously; they are given to the *Grand Seignor*, as presents of great value: and the number of these increaseth daily, as they are sent and presented by the *Tartars*,[4] by the *Bashaws*, and other great men, to the King and Queen. [They do likewise sometimes decrease, according as the *Grand Seignor* shall think fit. For upon diverse occasions and accidents, he causeth many of them to be turned out of this *Seraglio*, and to be sent into the old *Seraglio*: which is also a very goodly and spacious place, of which hereafter I shall take occasion to make mention.] These virgins, immediately after their coming into the *Seraglio*, are made *Turks*:[5] which is done by using this ceremony only; to hold up their forefinger, and say these words; *law illawheh illaw Allawh, Muhammed resoul Allawh.* That is, there is no God but God alone, and *Mahomet* is the messenger of God. And according as they are in age and disposition (being proved and examined by an old woman called *Kahiyah*

II OR 1200
WOMEN.

VIRGINS.

VIRGINS MADE
TURKS, AND HOW.

KAHIYAH CADUN, THE
MOTHER OF THE
MAIDS.

THEIR MANNER OF
LIFE.

CHAMBERS.

BEDS.

BAGNIOS.

SEWING, AND
CHESTS.

SCHOOLING, AND
MISTRESSES.

RECREATION.

Cadun,[6] that is, as we say, the mother of the maids) so they are placed in a room with the others of the same age, spirit, and inclination, to dwell and live together.

Now in the womens lodgings, they live just as nuns do in great nunneries. For these virgins have very large rooms to live in; and their bed-chambers will hold almost a hundred of them a-piece.[7] They sleep upon *Sofaes,* which are built longways on both sides of the room, and a large space left in the midst to go to and from about their business.

Their beds are very coarse and hard (for the *Turks* neither use feather-beds nor corded bed-steads) made of flocks of wool; and by every ten virgins there lies an old woman; and all the night long there are many lamps burning, so that one may see plainly throughout the whole room; which doth both keep the young wenches from wantonness, and serve upon any occasion which may happen in the night. Near unto the said bed-chambers they have their *Bagnios,* for their use at all times, with many fountains, out of which they are served with water; and, above their chambers, there are divers rooms, where they sit and sew, and there they keep their boxes and chests in which they lay up their apparel.

They feed by whole *Camaradaes,*[8] and are served and waited upon by other women: nor do they want any thing whatsoever, that is necessary for them.

There are other places likewise for them, where they go to school, to learn to speak and read, if they will, the *Turkish* tongue, to sew also, and to play on divers instruments: and so they spend the day with their mistresses, who are all ancient women; some hours, notwithstanding, being allowed them for their recreation, to walk in their gardens, and use such sports as they familiarly exercise themselves withall.

The King doth not at all frequent, or see, these

virgins, unless it be at that instant when they are first presented unto him; or else in case that he desire one of them for his bed-fellow, or to make him some pastime with musick, and other sports. Wherefore when he is prepared for a fresh mate, he gives notice to the said *Kahiya Cadun* of his purpose; who immediately bestirs herself like a crafty bawd, and chooseth out such as she judgeth to be the most amiable, and fairest of all; and having placed them in good order in a room, in two ranks, like so many pictures, half on the one side, and half on the other;

THE KING'S COMING TO THEM.

she forthwith brings in the King, who walking four or five times in the midst of them, and having view'd them well, taketh good notice within himself of her that he best liketh, but says nothing; only as he goeth

HIS CHOICE.

out again, he throweth a handkerchief into that virgin's hand;[9] by which token she knoweth that she is to lie with him that night. So she being, questionless, exceeding joyful to become the object of so great a fortune, in being chosen out from among so many to enjoy the society of an Emperor, hath all the art, that

PREPARATIVES.

possible may be, shewn upon her by the *Cadun*, in attiring, painting, and perfuming her; and at night she is brought to sleep with the *Grand Seignor* in the womens lodgings, where there are chambers set apart

BED-CHAMBER RITES.

for that business only. And, being in bed together, they have two great wax lights burning by them all night; one at the bed's feet, and the other by the door: besides there are appointed, by the *Cadun*, divers old *Blackmoor* women, to watch by turns that night in the chamber, by two at a time; one of them sits by the light at the bed's feet, and the other by the door; and when they will, they change, and other two supply their rooms, without making the least noise imaginable, so that the King is not any whit disturbed. Now in the morning when his Highness riseth (for he riseth first) he changeth all his apparel from top to toe, leaving those which he wore to her that he lay withall, and all the money that was in his pockets, were it never so much; and so departeth to his own lodgings; from whence also he sendeth her immediately a present of jewels, money, and vests of great value, agreeable to the satisfaction and content which he received from her that night. In the same manner he deals with all such as he maketh use of in that kind; but with some he continueth longer than with other some, and enlargeth his bounty far more towards some than others, according as his humour, and affection to them increaseth, by their fulfilling his lustful desires.

SULTANA QUEEN.

And if it so fall out, that any one of them doth conceive by him, and bring forth his first begotten child; then she is called by the name of *Sultana* Queen:[10] and if it be a son, she is confirmed and established by great feasts and solemnities; and forthwith hath a dwelling assigned unto her a-part, of many stately rooms well furnished; and many servants to attend upon her.

HER ALLOWANCE.

The King likewise alloweth her a large revenue, that she may give away, and spend at her pleasure, in whatsoever she may have occasion; and all they of the *Seraglio* must, and do acknowledge her for Queen, shewing all the duty and respect that may be, both to herself, and to them that belong unto her.

OTHER SULTANAS.

The other women (howsoever they bring forth issue) are not called Queens; yet they are called *Sultanas*, because they have had carnal commerce with the King: and she only is called Queen, which is the mother of the first begotten son, heir to the Empire; the which *Sultanas*, being frequented by the King at his pleasure, have also this prerogative; to be immediately removed from the common sort, and to live in rooms a-part, exceeding well served and attended; and have no want either of money, or apparel, in conformity to their degree.

All these *Sultanas* do resort together very familiarly, when they please; but not without great dissimulation, and inward malice; fearful lest the one should be better beloved of the *Grand Seignor* than the other; yet notwithstanding this their jealousy, they, in outward shew, use all kinds of courtesy one towards another.

Now if it happens that the first begotten son of the Queen, heir to the Empire, should die, and another of the *Sultanas* should have a second son; then, her son being to succeed the deceased heir, she is immediately made Queen:[11] and the former shall remain a *Sultana* only, and be deprived of the aforesaid revenue and royalty. Thus the title of Queen runneth from one *Sultana* to another, by virtue of the son's succession.

THE QUEEN CHANGED.

In times past the Queen was wont to be wedded to the King; but now she passeth without the *Kebin*,[12] that is, without an assignment of any jointure, or celebrating the nuptial rites; which is nothing else, but in the presence of the *Muftee* to give each of them their assent to matrimony, of which there is *Hoget* made (that is, an authentical writing or testification) not only of the consent of the two parties to be contracted, but also of the jointure which the King is to make over unto her.

NUPTIAL RITES.

The reason why the Queens are not now, nor have been of late years, espoused, is, not to dismember the King's patrimony of five hundred thousand chicquins a year. For *Sultan Selim* having allowed so much to the Empress his wife (to the end she might spend freely, and build churches[13] and hospitals, so that by all means she might be honoured and esteemed) made a decree, that all his successors should do the like, if so

THE QUEEN'S JOINTURE.

be they purposed to be married to their Queens. But now, the said revenue being otherwise employed, the *Bashaws* do endeavour, as much as in them lies, to keep the *Grand Seignor* from marrying; and so much the rather, because they would have none to rule but the King alone. Howsoever, married or not married, the mother of the heir is by every one called and acknowledged for Queen, and presented with many rich presents from all great personages; and hath

continually, at her gate, a guard of thirty or forty black eunuchs, together with the *Kuzlar Agha** their

**Kuzlar Agha
signifieth, master of
the virgins.*

master, whom she commandeth, and employeth in all her occasions; and so do all the other *Sultanas*, which never stir out of the *Seraglio*, but in company of the King himself, who oftentimes carrieth either all, or most of them abroad by water, to his other *Seraglios* of pleasure:[14] and in those ways through which they pass, to go to and fro from their *Kaiks*,† there is canvas

†*Barges. Canvas-
way.*

pitched up on both sides; and none may come near them but black *Eunuchs*, till they be settled, and covered close in the room at the stern of the *Kaik;*‡

‡*Barge.*

and then go in the bargemen; so that, in fine, they are never seen by any men, but by the *Grand Seignor* only, and the eunuchs.

 The King's daughters, sisters, and aunts, have their lodgings also in the same *Seraglio*; being royally served, and very sumptuously appareled, and live together by themselves, in continual pleasures; until such time as, at their request, the King shall be pleased to give them in marriage;[15] and then they come forth of that *Seraglio*, and carry, each of them, along with them a

chest which the *Grand Seignor* gives them, full of rich apparel, jewels, and money, to the value of, at the least, thirty thousand pounds *Sterling* a chest; and that is, as we call it, their portion.[16] They carry likewise along with them all that which they have hid from time to time, unknown to any but to themselves, amounting sometimes to a great matter, and stands them in good stead all their whole life-time. And if so be that they be in the *Grand Seignor's* favour, and that he be disposed to deal royally with them, then they are suffered to carry with them, out of the *Seraglio*, such women slaves as they please (provided they do not exceed the number of twenty a piece) and such eunuchs as they like best, for their service.

SLAVES AND
EUNUCHS.

These also, being called *Sultanas*, reserve still, as long as they live, their allowance of money which they had whilst they lived in the King's *Seraglio*, some a thousand, and some a thousand five hundred aspars[17] a day; the slaves also, and the eunuchs, do likewise enjoy their former pensions.

Their houses are furnished both with houshold stuff, and other necessary provision, from the King's *Hazineh** and *Begleek*,[†] that they may live *alla grande* like *Sultanas*; so that indeed they live far better, in every respect, without the *Seraglio*, than they did within it.

*Treasury.
†Store.

And if so be that a *Bashaw*, having married one of them, be not provided of a house fit for her, then the King giveth her one of his (for he hath many which fall to him by the death of great persons) that her house may be suitable with her greatness and quality.

BILL OF DOWRY.

Now, for the husband's part, he is, on the contrary, to make her a bill of dowry, ordinarily of at least a hundred thousand chicquins[18] in money, besides vests, jewels, brooches, and other ornaments, amounting to a great sum: for although the fashion of the *Sultanas* habit be common, and nothing different from that of the other women, yet the substance is far more rich and costly; the which redounds to the great charge and loss of their husbands.

PRIVATENESS.

They, being thus married, do not at all converse with men, more than they did when they lived in the

VISITINGS.

King's *Seraglio* (except with their own husbands) but
with women only; and that is commonly when they go
upon visits to see their old acquaintance in the *Seraglio*.
But because they themselves came forth from thence,
as I said before, they may not at their pleasure come
in again, without leave from the *Grand Seignor*.

THEY ARE THEIR
HUSBANDS
MASTERS.

*A dagger.

These *Sultanas*, the *Bashaws* wives, are, for the most
part, their husbands masters, insulting over them, and
commanding them as they please. They always wear at
their girdle a *Hanjar*,* set with rich stones, in token of
privilege and domination, and esteem of their
husbands, as of slaves; doing good or evil for them, as
they receive content and satisfaction from them, or as
they find them to be in favour and powerful with the
King. And sometimes they put their husbands away,
and take others; but not without the *Grand Seignor's*
leave: which divorce proves commonly to be the death
and ruin of the poor rejected husbands, [the King
being apt to give way to the will and persuasion of the
Sultanas: so it behoves them, in any case, to be very
obsequious to their wives.]

DIVORCE.

WHAT BECOMES OF
THE OTHER
WOMEN.

Now, the other women, which are not so fortunate
as to be beloved of the King, must still live together,
and diet with the rest of the young virgins, wasting
their youthful days amongst themselves, in evil
thoughts; for they are too strictly look'd unto, to
offend in act: and when they are grown old, they serve
for mistresses and overseers of the young ones, which
are daily brought into the *Seraglio*; but hold it their
best fortune (their former hopes of being bed-fellows
to an Emperor being now wholly frustrated) through
some accident to be sent forth from thence into the
old *Seraglio*; for from the old *Seraglio* they may be
married, if the mistress of that place give her consent
thereto, and may take with them such money as they,
through their frugality, have saved and spared of their

former allowance in the King's *Seraglio*, and such things as have been given them from time to time, which may amount to a reasonable value. For, whilst they are in the *Seraglio*, they get many things from the *Sultanas*, who, having formerly been companions with them, cannot but in some measure let them be partakers of their good fortune; besides their current pay out of the King's *Hazineh* of fifteen or twenty aspars* *per diem*, for the middle sort, and four or five *per diem* for the baser sort; the which is paid at every three months end, without any deferring or contradiction. In that manner also are the *Sultanas* paid, *viz.* quarterly, having for their shares from a thousand to a thousand five hundred aspars[†] a piece *per diem*, besides as much clothing as they will, and jewels in great abundance, given to them with the King's own hands.

[The soldiers likewise, and all such, of what quality soever they be, as are to receive pay from the *Grand Seignor*, are paid quarterly; and they call the first quarter's pay *Masar*, the second *Rejedg*, the third *Reshen*, and the fourth and last *Lezez*.]

The women servants have, besides their pay, two gowns of cloth a piece yearly, and a piece of fine linnen for smocks, of twenty *Pikes*[‡] long, and a piece more fine for handkerchiefs, of ten *Pikes*; and at the *Byram*[§] one silk gown a piece, and somewhat else, according to the liberality of the *Grand Seignor*, who, at that time above the rest, hath commonly a bountiful hand towards the women; giving to the *Sultanas* gowns with very rich furs, ear-rings, brooches, bodkins, bracelets for their arms and legs, and such like, set with stones of great worth; of all which the King hath continually great store, by reason of the unspeakable number of presents which are given unto him.

The *Sultanas* are likewise presented at such times by the *Bashaws*, and by the *Bashaws* wives (that by their

*That is, 9 *d.* or 12 *d.* a day.

MANNER OF THEIR PAY.

[†]That is, between 3 and 4 *l Sterling* a day.

CLOTHES AND JEWELS.

THE WOMEN SERVANTS ALLOWANCE.

[‡]A *Pike* is three quarters of a yard.
[§]Their great feast.

BYRAM-GIFTS.

SULTANAS PRESENTS.

means they may continue in grace and favour with the *Grand Seignor*) with most stately and rich gifts; and with money also, which indeed is more acceptable to them, than any other kind of present whatsoever. For they, being very covetous, do hoard up, and spend but sparingly, abandoning all manner of prodigality (in what may concern their own private purses) but warily and wittily provide against disasterous times, which may come upon them unawares; and especially against the King's death; for then (excepting the *Sultana* Queen, who remaineth still in the *Seraglio*, as being mother to the succeeding King) all the other poor desolate ladies lose the title of *Sultanas*, and are immediately sent to the old *Seraglio*; leaving behind them their sons and daughters, if they have any living, in the King's *Seraglio*, there to be kept, and brought up under the government and care of other women, appointed for that service. And in this case, finding themselves to be wealthy, they may marry with men of reasonable good quality, according to the measure of their portion or estate, which they possess; and the good-will, and good report of the mistress of the old *Seraglio* on their behalf, is none of the least furtherances and helps in that business. But the *Grand Seignor's* consent must be had thereto, notwithstanding; who will, for the most part, not only be made fully acquainted with the condition of their husbands, but also will know what jointure they will be content to make them, if in case they should put them away without their own consents, or otherwise leave them widows. Thus, by reason of their being turned out of the King's *Seraglio*, it is often seen, that though the daughter of the King be married to a *Bashaw*; yet the mother of that daughter, after the King's decease, must be content with a second husband of small account, far unequal, and much

FRUGALITY.

THE DAUGHTER
PREFERRED BEFORE
THE MOTHER.

55

inferior, both in title, wealth, and reputation, to her son in law.

The *Sultanas* have leave of the *Grand Seignor*, that certain *Jew*-women may at any time come into the *Seraglio* unto them; who being extraordinary subtil, and coming in under colour of teaching them some fine and curious needle works, or to shew them the art of making waters, oyls, and painting for their faces (having once made way with the better sort of the eunuchs which keep the gate, by often seeing them for their egress and regress) do make themselves by their crafty insinuations so familiar, and so welcome to the king's women, that, in a manner, they prevail with them in whatsoever they shall attempt for their own ends; for these are they whom the *Sultanas* do imploy in their private occasions; carrying out whatsoever they would have sold, and bringing in unto them any thing that they have a desire to buy. And hence it is, that all such *Jew*-women, as frequent the *Seraglio*, do become very rich; for what they bring in, they buy it cheap, and sell it dear to them: but on the contrary, when they have jewels or the like commodities to sell for the *Sultanas*, which are to be conveyed out by stealth, they receive a reasonable price for them of strangers, and then tell the simple ladies, who know not their worth, and are afraid to be discovered, that they sold them peradventure for the half of that which they had for them. And by this means there come things of great worth out of the *Seraglio*, to be sold abroad at easy rates: yet in the end the husbands of those *Jew*-women have but a bad market of it; for being discovered to be rich, and their wealth to be gotten by deceit, they oftentimes lose both goods and life too; the *Bashaws* and *Defterdars* altogether aiming at such as they are, thinking by that means to restore to the *Grand Seignor* that which hath from time to time

JEW-WOMEN.

THEIR ARTS.

THEIR FALSE DEALING.

ILL SUCCESS.

been stolen from him; [and the rather for that they themselves, under pretence of so good a work, may easily get shares in the estates of such delinquents.

But notwithstanding they are generally known, and accounted, for fraudulent and false-hearted people; yet there is scarcely a man of authority or esteem among the *Turks*, and especially the *Defterdars*, but hath a *Jew* for his counsellor, and assistant in the managing of his affairs; such a good opinion they have of their sufficiency, and so ready are the *Jews* to entertain any manner of imployment; so that their wives are not so great and powerful with the *Sultanas*, but they themselves are as intimate with the *Bashaws*, and other great ones of that rank.]

JEWS, COUNSELLORS TO GREAT MEN.

The women of the *Seraglio* are punished for their faults very severely, and extreamly beaten by their overseers; and if they prove disobedient, incorrigible, and insolent, they are by the king's order, and express command, turned out and sent into the old *Seraglio*, as being utterly rejected and cast off, and the best part of what they have is taken from them: but if they shall be found culpable of witchcraft, or any such like abomination; then they are bound hand and foot, and put into a sack, and in the night cast into the sea.[19] So that by all means it behoveth them to be very careful and obedient, and to contain themselves within the bounds of honesty and good behaviour, if they mean to prosper, and come to a good end.

PUNISHMENTS OF THE WOMEN BY BLOWS.

BY EXPULSION.

BY DEATH.

Now it is not lawful for any one to bring aught in unto them, with which they may commit the deeds of beastly and unnatural uncleanness; so that if they have a will to eat radishes, cucumbers, gourds, or such like meats; they are sent in unto them sliced, to deprive them of the means of playing the wantons: for they being all young, lusty, and lascivious wenches, and wanting the society of men, which would better

PREVENTION OF LUST.

instruct them, and questionless far better employ; them are doubtless of themselves inclined to that which is naught, and will often be possess'd with unchaste thoughts.

CHAPTER V

Of the Agiamoglans, *how taken, distributed, and imployed.*

*The word
signifieth unexpert
or untutor'd youths.

6 OR 700
AGIAMOGLANS.

AGIAMOGLANS ARE
RENEGADOS.

HOW THEY ARE
TAKEN.

Having already spoken of the women, I must in the next place say somewhat of the *Agiamoglans**[1] which are in the *Seraglio*, and of their imployments.

There are ordinarily about six or seven hundred of them,[2] from twelve to twenty five or thirty years of age, at the most, being all of them Christians children (as almost all *Agiamoglans* are) gathered every three years in *Morea*, and throughout all the parts of *Albania*:[3] the which renegado[4] children are disposed of, as hereafter you shall hear.

The number of them, which are to be taken, is uncertain; for there are gathered sometimes more and sometimes less, according as the *Capoochees* and officers appointed for that service, in their own discretion, shall think fit; but the greatest collection seldom or never comes to above two thousand.

They are taken from such families as are supposed to be of the best spirit, and most warlike disposition; nor may they, when they are gathered, exceed twelve, or fourteen years of age at the most,[5] lest they should be unfit for a new course of life, and too well settled in Christianity to become good *Turks*. The *Capooches* having finished their circuit, and gathered their whole complement, bring them forthwith to *Constantinople*, to be distributed and shared out as followeth. So soon as they are arrived at the port, they are all clothed in coarse *Salonichi* cloth,[6] it makes no matter of what colour; and their caps are of felt of the form of a sugar-loaf, of the colour of camel's hair; and so they are all brought to the *Vizir Azem*, who at that time is accompanied with the other *Bashaws*, and officers of the *Seraglio*; that he may make choice of the most well favoured, and such as he judgeth likely to prove the best spirits: then this choice being made, the said youths, chosen by the *Vizir*, are carried by the *Bustangee Bashaw* into the King's own *Seraglio*, and there distributed to such companies as want some to make up their compleat numbers. Then are they circumcised,[7] and made *Turks*, and set to learn the *Turkish* tongue; and according as their several inclinations are discovered and discerned by their overseers,[8] so are they encouraged in the same, and suffered to proceed: and such, as have a desire to learn, are taught to read and write; but generally all of them are taught to wrestle, to leap, to run, to throw the iron weight, to shoot the bow, to discharge a piece, and, to conclude, all such exercises as are befitting a *Turkish* soldier.

Now part of the residue of them are distributed by the chief *Vizir* into all the *Grand Seignor's* gardens, and houses of pleasure, and into such ships as sail for the King's account, and which go to lade wood, and such like provision for the *Seraglio*; confining them to the masters of the said vessels, with condition to restore them again, when he shall require them: and so he doth with the chief arts-men of the city, of all sorts of occupations, to the end that the youths may learn some trade, to keep them from idleness, when they are

HOW USED, AND APPARELED.

ELECTION OF THE BEST.

THEIR CIRCUMCISION.

SCHOOLING.

THE REST HOW DISPOSED.

become *Janizaries*, and are at home: or if they will, they may practise the said arts abroad, when they are at the wars, and reap great benefit for their pains. He lendeth likewise to all the *Bashaws*, and *Grandees* of the court, many of them to serve them; but they are all delivered by name and written down in a book, that he may have them returned again, when there shall be occasion to make them *Janizaries*. But these, which are given to the *Bashaws*, are the scum and refuse of all the rest, and are employed only in the service of stables, kitchins, and such base offices of drudgery; and the better sort of the residue are put into divers nurseries, committed to the custody and discipline of certain white eunuchs, who are appointed to be their overseers, and to take care that they be brought up, and trained in military exercises, until such time as they shall become fit to be entertained into the number of the *Janizaries*, in the room of the dead, or of old ones which are no longer fit for the wars, [but are made *Otooracks*,*9] and have leave to stay at home; so that these of the latter sort, kept in *Seminaries*, do indeed serve at all hands: the King, Queen, and *Vizir Azem*, imploying them also many times in their buildings, and other very laborious offices, without exception.

Milites emeriti, the word is derived from *Otooracks* which signifieth to sit down.

These *Agiamoglans* being thus distributed; the chief *Vizir* presents a book, wherein all their names are set down, to the King, who, having seen it, appointeth every one his pension, according to the *Canon*: which is of two or three, or at the most of five *Aspars* a day; and underwrites it with his own hand: the which book is forthwith consigned into the custody of the chief *Defterdar*: that so he seeing by the said book what their several names and pensions are, they may duly receive their pay from him. Now this *Defterdar* is bound, so often as their pay is due, that is once in three months,

BOOK AND
PENSION.

to visit them all if he can; inquiring who is dead, and taking good notice how the others live and spend their time; whether they profit or not, by their tutors and overseers; that if so be things be not as they should be, he may acquaint the *Grand Seignor* therewith, and have them amended.[10]

I will now return to speak of the *Agiamoglans* of the *Seraglio*; having not thought it superfluous to have digressed a little, and to have spoken somewhat of the other *Agiamoglans* also: for it may peradventure prove delightsome to those who have not as yet heard of those passages so distinctly.

AGIAMOGLANS OF THE *SERAGLIO* HOW USED.

The *Agiamoglans* of the *Seraglio*, albeit they are chosen for the best uses, out of the rest, by the chief *Vizir*; yet are their first imployments but very base and slavish. For they serve in the stables, kitchins, gardens, for digging, for cleaving of wood; and are made to row

*Barges.

in *Kaiks*,* and to lead the greyhounds a coursing, and whatsoever else they are commanded to do, by their

†Heads of the companies of *Agiamoglans*.

Oda Bashaws:† the which *Oda Bashaws* are also *Agiamoglans* as they are, but of the highest rank and longest standing, and have about fifteen aspars a day;

ODA BASHAWS WAGES.

two vests of cloth yearly; two pieces of linnen cloth for shirts and handkerchiefs; and so much sattin or fine cloth as will make each of them a pair of *Chakshirs* or breeches, after their fashion down to the heels, and ruffled in the small of the leg, as our boots are. Nevertheless these *Oda Bashaws* are all under command

GOVERNMENT.

of the *Kahiyah*, who is the *Bustangee Bashaw's* steward; now the *Bustangee Bashaw* himself hath daily about three hundred aspars pay; for he is their patron, judge, and protector. [And as any *Turk* whatsoever may be known of what degree he is, by the bigness and making up of the turbant which he wears, and by some other tokens which they observe in their habit; so to the end that

‡These and *Oda Bashaws* are of equal authority.

the *Oda Bashaws* and *Bulook Bashaws*‡ may be known

from the common sort of *Agiamoglans*,] they wear broad silken girdles of divers colours about their middles, and are allowed a larger stipend: who, by authority given them from the *Kahiyah*,* do bring the underlings to such an extraordinary subjection and sufferance, by their often beating them upon the least misdemeanor; that they do not only not refuse all manner of pains taking, but patiently undergo whatsoever is done unto them.

*Bustangee Bashaw's steward.

SLAVERY.

They have their terms and prerogatives amongst themselves; preceding or succeeding one another according to the length of time which they have spent in the *Seraglio*: so that in process of time, if they still continue there, and are not sent out upon other occasions, they may aspire to the degree of chief steward to the *Bustangee Bashaw*, or of *Bustangee Bashaw* himself, which is a very eminent place; for he hath the keeping of all the *Grand Seignor's* garden houses, and steers the King's *Kaik*,[†11] and weareth a turbant upon his head in the *Seraglio*, altho' he were but lately an *Agiamoglan* as the rest are, and did wear one of the aforesaid felt caps: who also (if he be in grace with the King, as commonly every *Bustangee Bashaw* is) may rise to greater dignities, as to be captain *Bashaw*, *Bashaw* of *Cairo*, *Damascus*, *Aleppo*, etc. nay sometimes to be *Vizir Azem*.

POSSIBILITY OF PREFERMENT.

†Barge.

These *Agiamoglans* are not altogether debarred from liberty, and going abroad, but may upon good occasion be licensed to go whither they please,[12] although at the first they are strictly look'd unto: and the *Bustangee Bashaw* always takes with him good store of them, when by his Majesty's order he is sent to put some great man to death: the which is commonly done by the hands of four or five of the chiefest, and strongest of the said *Agiamoglans*.

SOME *TURKS* AMONG THEM.

There are sometimes natural born *Turks* brought in

amongst them, but indeed very seldom, by means made to the *Bustangee Bashaw*, who therein doth greatly pleasure such poor folks as are willing to be rid of their children: but it must be first made known to the *Grand Seignor*, and done with his consent. [For the natural born *Turks* are not held to be of so brave spirits, and fit for service, as the other: and for divers other respects best known to themselves, as the increasing the number of *Mussulmen*,* and the like, they do not willingly admit of any but Christians children.]

*True believers.

THEIR ROOMS.

Their rooms, bagnoes, and kitchins, are joined to the walls of the *Seraglio* without; divided severally, and equally, for each company of them, and built for the more commodity of such offices and services, as the said *Agiamoglans* are appointed for.

THEIR DIET.

And as for their diet, they order it as they please, having flesh and pulse for their pottage; their bread also, and every thing for their food, delivered unto them daily from the *Keeler*,[†13] and the dressing of it left to themselves. Now for that many of them lie near the sea-side, they take good store of fish, part of which they sell, and reserve the rest for their own eating.

†Buttery.

THEIR SLEEPING.

They sleep always in their cloths, putting off only their uppermost coat, and their shoes, according to the ordinary custom of the poorer sort of *Turks*; between a couple of rugs in the winter, and thin blankets in the summer.

They never see the King, unless it be when he passeth through the gardens, or when he taketh boat, or else when he goeth a hunting; for he makes them serve instead of hounds to find out his game: but when his Majesty will be in the gardens to take his pleasure, and make pastime with his concubines, then all the *Agiamoglans* being warned by an eunuch, who crieth aloud *Helvet*,[‡14] do presently get out with all

‡A word commanding absence, and retiring: never used but for the King.

speed at the gates by the sea-side, where they may walk upon the banks and causeys, but must not dare to go in again until the King and his women be departed: for there may none come near, nor be in sight of them, but himself and his black eunuchs: nay if any other should but attempt, by some trick in creeping into some private corner, to see the women, and should be discovered, he should be put to death immediately. Every one therefore, so soon as they hear *Helvet* cried, runs out of sight as far as they can, to be free from all fear and suspicion.

NONE MAY SEE THE KING'S WOMEN.

Now of this rank of *Agiamoglans* which are in the King's *Seraglio*, they never make *Janizaries*, as they do of those which are brought up in the other *Seraglios* and Seminaries; and of such as are lent to divers of the King's subjects, as tradesmen, masters of ships, and the like, and to the *Bashaws*: but his Majesty's turn being served of these, he bestows them upon his gentlemen *Aghas*, when he imploys them abroad in some principal government, that they may be faithful assistants unto them in their businesses, and that in time they themselves may become men of worth; as often they do, if by their diligence, and fidelity, they prove to be men of good desert.

THE *JANIZARIES* ARE MADE OF *AGIAMOGLANS* IN OTHER SEMINARIES.

OTHER USES OF THEM.

The *Grand Seignor* likewise maketh great use of them, when he intendeth a journey to any place; as when he goeth to the wars, or any whither else, far from *Constantinople*; for the pitching of his tents, for removing, and carrying of chests and baskets, and many other such like services, as must be done at those times: for which imployments the King never takes with him less than three or four hundred of them.[15]

CHAPTER VI

*This word
signifieth, youths
with in: and they are
so called, because
they are reserved for
the service of the
King's person.

Of the King's Itchoglans,* their severe discipline, and education in four Subordinate Schools; and of their after advancements.

ITCHOGLANS.

It now remaineth that I say somewhat of the *Grand Seignor's Itchoglans;*[1] which are youths kept also in the *Seraglio*, but in far better fashion than the *Agiamoglans*; and are, for the King and country's service, brought up in learning, in the knowledge of the laws, and in military exercises; that they may in time be made able to perform those things, which belong to the government of the whole empire. And albeit for the most part these are Christian captives and renegados, yet there are some natural born *Turks* amongst them, (which must be youths of very comely aspect, and their outsides must promise a great deal of worth and goodness) brought in by the *Capee Agha's* means, who is chief chamberlain, with the King's consent: but this happeneth very seldom, and is effected with great difficulty; for the ancient institution was, that the *Itchoglans* should always be made of christian renegados, and captives only, of the most civil and noblest that could be found.

TURKS, HARDLY
ADMITTED.

NOBLE CAPTIVES.

Wherefore, when in the wars, either by sea or land, it happens, that any youth is taken, who is discovered to be of noble parents and comely personage; or if any such voluntarily come and offer himself to become

Turk (as divers have done in hope of advancement) he is presently mark'd, and set apart for the *Grand Seignor*; and is, so soon as he is thought capable and apprehensive, instructed in matters of government, being as it were ordained for great imployments. Now such are of very great esteem: for the *Turks* themselves affirm, that nobleness of birth cannot but produce the most virtuous and generous spirits; especially when it is seconded and accompanied with good education, which is professed in the *Seraglio*, where there is great severity used in all the orders of discipline, the government of them being in the hands of the masters, who are all white eunuchs for the most part, and very rough and cruel in all their actions; insomuch that their proverb faith, that when one cometh out of that *Seraglio*, and hath run through all the orders of it, he is, without all question, the most mortified and patient man in the world. For the blows which they suffer, and the fastings which are commanded them for every small fault, are to be admired; nay, some of them are so cruelly handled; that although their time of being in the *Seraglio* be almost expired, and that they should in a few years come forth to be made great men; yet, not being able to endure such cruelty any longer, they procure to be turned out, contenting themselves with the title, and small pay of a *Spahee* or a *Mutaferraka*, rather than be so often punished and made weary of their lives, in expectation of greater preferments.

The number of these *Itchoglans* is uncertain, for there are sometimes more, and sometimes less of them; but as I have heard, they are commonly about a hundred, the *Grand Seignor* being very willing to entertain all such as are given him of the aforesaid quality, be they never so many; provided they be young when they are first brought unto him.

EUNUCHS CRUEL.

PUNISHMENTS.

THEIR NUMBER.

The course that is taken with them, so soon as they come into the *Seraglio*, is admirable, and nothing resembling the barbarism of *Turks*, but beseeming men of singular virtue and discipline. For they are exceeding well entered, and daily taught, as well good fashion and comely behaviour, as they are instructed in the rites and ceremonies of the *Mahometan* law, or whatsoever else may tend to the enriching of their minds.

And for this purpose they have rooms, which the *Turks* call Odas,* but we may more properly, in regard of the use they are put unto, call them schools: of which there are four, the one taking degrees from the other. Now into the first they all come when they are but children, where the primary precept they learn is silence; then their personal postures, against such time as they shall be about the King, which is, that they hold down their heads, and look downwards with their hands before them joined across; all which betokeneth singular reverence.[2]

They, by a white eunuch, who is chief over all the other masters, and ushers, they are set to learn to write and read; to practise the *Turkish* tongue; and are taught their prayers in the *Arabian* tongue by heart. And in this *Oda* they are both morning and evening so diligently followed, and carefully look'd unto, that by report it is a thing of admiration. Now in this first school they usually stay about five or six years; and such as are dull, and hard of apprehension, stay longer.[3]

But by the way, before I come to the next, I may not omit to tell you, that so soon as they are given to the King, before they are of the first *Oda*, they are register'd by their *Turkish* names in a book, and the names of their native countries set down with them; the *Grand Seignor* allowing them a small pension of four or

DISCIPLINE IN RELIGION AND CIVILITY.

Oda signifieth a chamber, or room.

FOUR *ODA* SCHOOLS.

FIRST SCHOOL.

FIRST LESSON IS SILENCE.

SECOND, REVERENCE.

THIRD, TO WRITE AND READ, AND SPEAK *TURKISH*; AND SAY THE *ARABIAN* PRAYERS BY HEART.

BOOK OR CHECK-ROLL.

five aspars a day;[4] the copy of which book is also sent to the great *Defterdar*, that every one of them may in due time, that is quarterly, have the aforesaid pension sent unto them.

SECOND SCHOOL.

FOURTH, RHETORICK, *PERSIAN, ARABIAN*, AND *TARTARIAN* TONGUES.

From the first *Oda* they are removed to the second, where, by more learned and sufficient tutors than the former, they are taught the *Persian, Arabian*, and *Tartarian* tongues; and take great pains in reading divers authors, that they may be the better able to speak the *Turkish* elegantly; which cannot be done without some knowledge, and good insight in those three tongues, upon which the *Turkish* chiefly doth depend; and indeed there is found a great difference between their speech, and that of the vulgar sort.[5]

FIFTH, BODILY EXERCISES.

Here also they begin to learn to wrestle, to shoot in the bow,[6] to throw the iron mace, to toss the pike, to run, and to handle their weapons, etc. And in these exercises in their several orders and several places, they spend whole hours; being severely punished if they shall in any wise seem to grow negligent.

They spend likewise other five or six years in this *Oda*; whence, being become men, strong, and fit for any thing, they are removed to the third *Oda*; where,

THIRD SCHOOL.

SIXTH, HORSE-MANSHIP AND ACTIVITY.

forgetting nothing of what they learned before, but greatly increasing their knowledge, they also learn to ride, and how to behave themselves in the wars.

SEVENTH, TRADES.

Moreover, every one of them, according as he is thought fit for it, here learns a trade, necessary for the service of the King's person, *videlicet*, to shave, to make up a turbant, to fold up apparel handsomely, to pair nails, to attend at the *Bagno*, to keep hawks, and land-spaniels, to be sewers, querries of the stable, target-bearers, to wait at table, and the like: as hereafter I shall shew, so that, having been in these offices a few years, they become men able to teach others.

But, whilst they are in these three schools, they are

but meanly appareled, having yearly their two vests of cloth somewhat fine, but their linnen is such as the *Agiamoglans* wear.

The punishments also, which they suffer in this *Oda*, are extream, for their masters often give them an hundred blows with a cudgel upon the soles of their feet and buttocks, insomuch that they leave them oftentimes for dead.[7]

Neither are they permitted, so long as they are in these three *Odas*, to be familiar with any but themselves, and that with great modesty too;[8] so that it is a matter of great difficulty for any stranger to

speak with them, or see them; which if it be obtained, it must be by express leave from the *Capee Agha*, who causeth an *Eunuch*[9] to be there present, so long as any stranger shall be in the company of the said youths. Nay, when they have occasion to go to the *Bagno*, or the like businesses, the eunuchs are always at hand, that so by all means they may be kept from lewdness.[10]

And in their bed-chambers, which are long rooms, and hold about thirty or forty in each of them, (for they sleep near one another upon the *Sofas*,) there are every night lamps burning, and eunuchs lying by them to keep them in awe, and from leud and wanton behaviour.

In the third *Oda*, some of them do also learn ordinary Mechanick arts, as sewing in leather, (which is in great use and esteem amongst the *Turks*) to mend guns, to make bows and arrows, and quivers, and the like; from which trades they often have both their sirname and their reputation too. For they are much made of, who will be diligent, and fly idleness; holding it rather an honour, than an ignominy, to have a trade. [For therein they imitate the *Grand Seignors* themselves, who, for good example sake, in their youth are taught some trade or other; which although they never practise when they are Kings,[11] yet they are willing their subjects should know that they are able to do it, if they please. And divers great men, nay, *Bashaws* themselves, both have been, and are to this day called by the names of such arts, as they practised, when they were in this *Oda*.]

Here also the eunuchs, their tutors, make trial of their constancy in religion, searching, as far as in them lies, their hearts, to see how they stand affected to *Turcism*. For the time growing near, wherein they are to pass to the fourth *Oda*, which is the chiefest and last, and from which they are called to business of great importance, they would not then have them at all remember that they were formerly Christians, or to have the least desire imaginable to turn to their first belief; lest that they should in time, by some stratagems and politick courses, peradventure prove disadvantageous to the *Turkish* empire. So then all possible proof and trial being made, and they found to be strongly persuaded of the truth of that religion; they then are preferred to the fourth *Oda*, where they are once more register'd. For all they, which are of the third *Oda*, are not translated to the fourth at one and the same time; but only such as have gone through all the degrees of discipline in the three former, and are become fit for service. And there is a note kept apart of them, which come into this fourth *Oda*. For they are immediately ordained for the *Grand Seignor's* own service, and have their pay increased some more, and some less, unto eight[12] aspars a day, and their habit changed from cloth to silk and cloth of gold of great price.[13]

Now here their punishments cease: but they continue still with their heads and beards shaven; only they suffer some locks to grow on each side, from their temples; which hang down below their ears, for

THEY TAKE THEIR *COGNOMINA* FROM TRADES.

TRIAL OF RELIGION.

FOURTH SCHOOL.

PREFERMENTS.

PUNISHMENTS CEASE.

NEATNESS.

a sign that they are the next which are capable of the preferment of coming into the King's chamber.

They must be very cleanly, and neat in their apparel, before they come about the *Grand Seignor's* person; many of them ever accompanying his Majesty when he goes abroad upon pleasure, provided none of his women be with him. And they may now freely converse with all the great men of the *Seraglio*, and with the *Bashaws* also; and are often presented with gifts by men of the best quality, to insinuate into their favour; hoping that they one day may become men of great command, and so be able to stand them in stead in their occasions.

Now out of these young men of the fourth *Oda*, after they have finished the appointed term of years, and have been made perfect in all things as aforesaid, the King chooseth his *Aghas*, which are his gentlemen, that attend only upon him; whose names, and places, are as follow.

1. The *Silihtar Agha*; the King's sword bearer.
2. The *Chiohadar Agha*; he which carrieth his *Yagmoorlick*.
3. The *Rechiubtar Agha*; yeoman of the stirrup.
4. The *Mataragee Agha*; he which brings him water to wash his hands and face.
5. The *Telbentar Agha*; he which brings him his *Turbant*.
6. The *Kembasir Agha*; he which looketh to his apparel, and the washing of his linnen.
7. The *Cheshneghir Bashaw*; the chief sewer.
8. The *Dogangee Bashaw*; the chief falconer.
9. The *Zagargee Bashaw*; the chief huntsman.
10. The *Turnackgee Bashaw*; he which paireth the King's nails.
11. The *Berber Bashaw*; chief barber.
12. The *Hamawmgee Bashaw*; he which washeth the

King in the *Bagno*.

13.   The *Muhasabegee Bashaw*; the chief accountant.

14.   The *Teskeregee Bashaw*; his Majesty's secretary.[14]

All which are made of the eldest sort of the *Itchoglans* of the fourth *Oda*; and these are always in his Majesty's presence, holding down their heads, for they may not be so bold as to look him in the face, and standing with their hands across before him, in token of reverence and humility. Nor may they presume at all to speak to the *Grand Seignor*, nor in his presence to one another: but if the King shall command, or call for aught, they are wonderful speedy, and ready to obey. They all do execute their offices distinctly, as aforesaid, and attend in places appointed for them, that they may be the better able to perform their several duties, and the more ready to obey at every beck. At the hours of dinner and supper they wait in the room, taking the meat from the hands of the under-*Sewer* at the door, and so his Majesty's table being made ready, which is of a *Bulgar* hide,[15] upon a *Sofa*, they bring in meat, which is set thereon orderly dish by dish, by the chief *Sewer*, before the King, and is taken off again as his Majesty shall appoint.

The *Grand Seignor* is very well pleased with these *Aghas*, and takes great delight in their service and company, for that they are, as I may say, of his own planting, making them ride on horse-back, and playing with them at several sports, especially at the *Jereet*,* at such times as he is well disposed; every gracing them with bestowing gifts on them, of vests, swords, bows, and the like, and oftentimes ready money: all which came before to the King's hands by way of gift. Now besides those favors, his Majesty at convenient times useth to bestow upon them the dispatching of ambassies for foreign parts; which is a merchandise held by them to be of a great price, and bringeth no small

GESTURE.

WAITING.

GREAT *TURK'S* TABLE.

EXERCISES.

*A kind of running at base on horse-back, darting lances one at another.

GIFTS.

AMBASSAGES CONFERRED.

profit into their purses. For one of them having his commission from the *Grand Seignor* for such or such a Prince, howbeit it is not intended that he should go, presently informs himself what that Prince usually doth present the Ambassador withal; and so accordingly agreeth with a *Chiaush* or with one of such like quality, to undertake the ambassage; who must give for the same, as they two can agree between themselves; either in ready money before his departure, or otherwise at his return, as the *Agha* shall think best for his profit; and so forthwith he gives expedition to the party chosen.

VASSAL PRINCES.

*Moldavia.

This kind of imployment proves wonderfully beneficial. For in the establishing of the Princes of *Walachia, Bugdania,** Transilvania*, and of the King of *Tartary*, to all which Princes the *Grand Seignor* sendeth Ambassadors for confirming their possession of the said dominions, they, which are sent, receive great benefit; it being specified in their *Canon*, how much every one is to disburse for being honoured with that

†Displaced; or turned out of office.

solemnity; [though peradventure they be *Maazold*† again, before they be scarce warm in their places.]

And this the King doth of policy, to the end his gentlemen may become rich, laying up money to serve for their necessary expences, and furnishing them by that means with divers things, against such time as they shall go forth of the *Seraglio*; which is as often as his Majesty thinks fit, and that most commonly on a sudden; either to be general at sea, Bashaw of *Messur*,‡ *Halep*,§ *Shawm*,¶ *Babylon*, or of some other such great cities, which have whole provinces under them. The *Grand Seignor* gives also to each of them, when he sends them forth upon any of the aforesaid imployments, a *Musahib*,‖ that is in effect, a helping companion; such an one as shall have liberty freely to talk with him, and go out and in unto him when he pleaseth: the which

THEIR GOING FORTH OF THE *SERAGLIO* TO THE CHIEF OFFICES.

‡*Cairo.*

§*Aleppo.*

¶*Damascus.*

‖The word signifieth, a familiar talker or discourser.

MUSAHIB.

title, and favour of being made *Musahib* to any of the *Aghas*, proves to be of so great reputation, that it is esteemed above any other sort of imployment. For as it is hard to be obtained, so it is only bestowed upon such subjects as have deserved well at the King's hands.

A POLITICK COURSE.

And this hath been a course used of old, by the *Grand Seignor's* progenitors, that they may have some trusty subjects abroad, to give notice to the *Port* of the carriage of the *Bashaws* in their several regiments, or of any other; if so be they should attempt any thing that might be prejudicial to the crown; that so the King by cutting off their provision, and the like, may easily anticipate their plots and designs.

OTHER OFFICES.

But if his Majesty be not pleased, or the occasion do not require, so highly to exalt some one of the aforesaid *Aghas*, as to be of the degrees already named; he then makes him *Beglerbeg* of *Græcia*, or of *Natolia*; *Agha* of the *Janizaries*; *Spaheeler Aghajee*, which is head over all the *Spahees*; *Imrohor Bashaw*, which is master of the horse; or at the least a *Capoochee Bashaw*, which is head over the *Capoochees*.

The *Grand Seignor* having bestowed any of the said places upon them, they forthwith leave the *Seraglio*, and carry with them all their estates, both money and goods; and oftentimes take with them other young men of the other *Odas*, who are permitted to go, through their own hastiness, and great importunity, not being willing to stay out their time, but, losing the King's favour, are content with small pay, and lesser reputation, to go along with the said *Aghas*.

Such as are to go out, upon the greatest im-ployments, are accompanied forth of the King's *Seraglio* by the *Vizir Azem*; who also presenteth them, and giveth them entertainment for three or four days in his house, until such time as they can be provided of houses of their own, whither afterwards they repair, and set their families in order; taking also unto them such as are come out of the *Seraglio* with them for assistants, and ministers, in the charge assigned unto them. They also accept of the service of strangers, who come in by gifts; which likewise redounds to the benefit and advantage of the great ones.

ORDER IN
SUCCESSION.

They which succeed in preferment those that are gone out of the *Seraglio*, upon the aforesaid im-ployments, are, as the custom commandeth, such as are next in years unto them, and of the longest residence. Nor can this course be altered, unless by some sinister accident or evil behaviour they fail thereof: so that it is always known amongst themselves, who is next capable of publick imployment; nay, the business is so orderly carried, and their course so regular, that even they of the third *Oda* do know what their future fortunes will be, if they live to enjoy them. And indeed all of them live in continual hope, and desire, that the *Grand Seignor* would often be pleased to send them abroad; that so they may the sooner be out of their hard service in the *Seraglio*, and enter into the state of ample government. [It is no marvel then the *Turkish* officers are so often changed, seeing that every *Grand Seignor* hath so many servants of his own, that seek for advancement.]

They are most commonly of five and thirty, or forty years of age, before they are sent abroad: and, because they come out of the *Seraglio* with their beards shaven, they are fain to stay within doors, for some days, to let them grow, that they may be fit to come amongst other great men; with which staying at home they are very well contented. For in that time they receive the presents which are sent them from all the *Sultanas*, of vests, shirts, linnen breeches, and handkerchiefs of all sorts, richly wrought and of great

PRESENTS FROM
GREAT PERSONS
WHILST THEY STAY.

worth; and from the *Bashaws* and other great men, horses, carpets, vests, slaves, and other things, fit for the erecting and furnishing of an house and family; the which presents are made the greater, and richer, by so much the more as the party, to whom they are given, is known to be favoured and beloved of the King.

COMING ABROAD
AND VISITINGS.

Now so soon as their beards are grown, they go abroad, and begin their visits; first, to the chief *Vizir*, and then in order to the other great ones, till they have been with them all; and last of all, offer their service to the *Capee Agha* in all humble manner,

CAPEE AGHA VISITED.

acknowledging that all their best fortunes and honours have been conferred upon them by his means, and promising for ever all dutiful respect unto him for the same.

But this compliment with the *Capee Agha* is performed, without the gate on the King's side, which is kept by the white eunuchs; for they may not come any more within that gate, unless they be called for by the King, for to treat of things belonging to their imployments, before their departure.

They all strive to gain the love and good will of the *Capee Agha*, that he may be as a protector, and patron unto them, and that, when they are absent, he may

THE POWER OF THE
CAPEE AGHA.

possess the *Grand Seignor* with a good opinion of them; for they know he is very powerful with him, being the chiefest in the *Seraglio*, and always nearest to the King.

CHAPTER VII

Of inferior persons, as Buffons, Mutes, Musicians; of the white Eunuchs, and of the Grand Officers of the Seraglio.

B esides the women, and the *Agiamoglans* of this *Seraglio*, and the aforesaid youths the *Itchoglans* last spoken of, there are many other ministers for all manner of necessary services. There are also *Buffons*,* and such as shew tricks, musicians, wrestlers, and many *Mutes*[†1] both old and young; who have liberty to go in and out at the King's gate, with leave only of the *Capee Agha*. It is worthy the observation, that in the *Seraglio* both the *Grand Seignor*, and divers that are about him, can reason and discourse with the *Mutes* of any thing, as well and as distinctly, *alla Mutescha*, by nods and signs, as they can with words; a thing well befitting and suiting with the gravity of the better sort of *Turks*, who cannot endure much babbling. Nay, the *Sultanas* also, and many other of the King's women do practise it, and have many dumb women and girls about them for that purpose.

This hath been an ancient custom in the *Seraglio*, to get as many *Mutes*, as they can possibly find; but chiefly for this one reason, which is, that they hold it a thing unbefitting the *Grand Seignor*, and not to suit with his greatness, to speak to any about him familiarly; wherefore he takes this course, that he may

*Jesters.

†Dumb men.

DISCOURSE BY SIGNS.

79

the more tractably and domestically jest, and talk with the *Mutes*, and with others that are about him, to make him pleasant, with diversity of pastime.

A FURTHER USE OF THEM.

[The King, besides that, makes another use of them; and that is this, when his Majesty shall resolve with himself to put a *Vizir* to death, or some one of that rank; and that he be willing to see it done with his own eyes in the *Seraglio*; he then having called him into one of his rooms, and holding him in discourse whilst his *Mutes* are in readiness (the poor man peradventure suspecting nothing) he makes but a sign unto them, and they presently fall upon him, and strangle him, and so draw him by the heels out of the gates.

MUTES STRANGLE MEN IN THE *SERAGLIO*.

But that which, in my opinion, is admirable in these *Mutes* (who being born deaf, and so of necessity must remain dumb) is, that many of them can write, and that very sensibly and well: now how they should learn without the sense of hearing, I leave to others judgments; but I am sure I have seen it, and have myself made answer to them in writing.]

MUTES CAN WRITE.

It followeth now that I speak of the white eunuchs, who as the black ones are for the service and attendance of the *Sultanas*, and for the keeping of their gate; so are the white eunuchs appointed for the King, and his gate. But there are four ancient and principal men amongst them, which attend only the most trusty and important imployments, both about the King's person, and his houshold. Of which, the first is the *Capee Agha*, for he is the principal of all the white *eunuchs*, and is chamberlain: the second is the *Hazinehdar Bashaw*, the treasurer of the house: the third is the *Keelerge Bashaw*, the chief butler, and master of the wardrobe: the fourth is the *Sarai Agasee*, the keeper of the *Seraglio*.

WHITE EUNUCHS.

FOUR PRINCIPAL EUNUCHS IN THE *SERAGLIO*.

First and chiefest; the *Capee Agha* or chamberlain.
2. Treasurer of the house.
3. Master of the wardrobe.
4. The Keeper of the house.

Of these four old eunuchs, the *Capee Agha*, as I said,

is chief in authority, and in greatest esteem with the *Grand Seignor.* For none but he can of himself speak with his Majesty, neither can any messages, writings, or petitions be sent in, ordinarily, but by his hand and means. He likewise doth always accompany the King's person, withersoever he goeth, both without, and within the *Seraglio.* And when he goeth to his women also, he waiteth upon him to the very door, which leadeth in unto them: but there he stoppeth, and so returns to his own lodgings again; ever leaving somebody to wait at the said door, that, when the King is ready to come away from them, they may call him. The *Capee Aghas* ordinarily pension is eight*[2] *Sultanas*† a day, besides vests, and other necessaries, as many, as he will. He also gets great store of money (and indeed, more than befits a man, that hath so small occasion of expence, as he hath), by virtue of his place. For that, both they of the *Seraglio,* and those abroad, of what condition or degree soever they be, to obtain his favour, and furtherance in any business, present him with all that they can imagine may give him content, whatsoever it cost.

HIS PENSION.

*About 3 *l. sterling.*

†They are called *Sultanas*, because they are coined at *Constantinople,* where the *Sultan* lives: they are worth about 7 *s.* 10 *d.* a piece.

PRESENTS.

THE TREASURER.

The second is, the *Hazinehdar Bashaw,* and he hath the charge, and keeping of the treasury, which is within the *Seraglio;* he having one key of it, and the *Grand Seignor* another; the door being likewise sealed with the King's seal, which is never taken off, but when the King himself gives order for the opening of the same. In this *Hazineh* are all the treasures, which have been laid up by the deceased Emperors; and into this cometh no other revenue of the crown, than that from *Egypt,* and the adjacent provinces, of six hundred thousand chicquins† yearly, all the other revenues going into the outward *Hazineh;* out of which all expences are born, both ordinary and extraordinary: but there is not aught taken out of the aforesaid

TREASURE.

‡240 thousand pounds *sterl.*

OUTWARD TREASURY.

inward *Hazineh*, unless it be upon extream necessity, when the *Grand Seignor* is not otherwise provided, to appease the outcries and threatenings of the soldiers for their pay, or for some other the like occasion; and this ought to be done with this *proviso*, that the *Grand Defterdar* be bound to make it good again to the utmost aspar; but I suppose they have not of late been able to perform it.

HOUSHOLD
TREASURER'S
OFFICE.

This *Agha* must keep an exact account of all the treasure that is brought in, or taken out of the same; nor may any go into the said *Hazineh*, but only he himself, and such as he shall take in with him, when occasion shall require. And when there is any gold or silver taken out, it is all put into leather bags, and so brought unto the King, who disposeth thereof as he thinketh fit.

He hath also the custody of all the King's jewels, of which he keepeth a book by himself, that he may know what jewels the King gives away, what jewels are given to the King, and what are likewise for his Majesty's own wearing; and, the *Capee Agha* dying, he succeeds him in his place.

MASTER OF THE
WARDROBE.

The third, which is the *Keelergee Bashaw*, keeps the King's wardrobe; into which are brought all the presents which are given to the *Grand Seignor*, as cloth of gold, plate, silks, woollen clothes, furs of all sorts, swords, brooches, raw silk, carpets, and whatsoever else may serve for his Majesty's use, either to keep or give away. Of all which things he keeps particular notes and inventories, to the end he may also at any time see what is given to the King, and what the King gives away to others; the which is a very painful imployment, inasmuch as his Majesty doth, every day, as well take as give a great number of vests and other such like things. But the business is so well ordered and carefully look'd unto, that there doth not follow

BUSY IMPLOYMENT.

any confusion at all. This eunuch hath many servants under him, and stays always, for the most part, within the *Seraglio*: his pension is a thousand aspars* a day, besides vests and other such gifts, which are given him in abundance from time to time: he also is much favoured, and graced by the King, for that he is to succeed the *Hazinehdar Bashaw*, in case the said *Hazinehdar* should die, or change his place: and is well esteemed of, and reverenced by all, as well without, as within the *Seraglio*.

HIS PENSION.

*50 *s. sterl.* at 20 aspars the shilling.

The fourth and last, which is the *Sarai Agasee*, hath charge to look unto the *Seraglio*; nor doth he ever go out of it, especially in the *Grand Seignor's* absence; but is very vigilant, not only in seeing all things prepared for the daily service of the same, but also to look over all the rooms, and see that they be well kept; and to eye the officers, and servants of the house, marking whether they exercise themselves, or no, in their several functions. Now because he is ancient, and his businesses great, he hath liberty to ride within the *Seraglio*, about the courts, and gardens, and by the sea-side, as the three former *Aghas* are also permitted to do; for which purpose they have a stable of horses in a garden, for their use alone.

KEEPER OF THE *SERAGLIO*.

HIS LIBERTY.

His pension is eight hundred aspars† a day, besides an allowance of vests, and furs, as many as he can well have occasion to wear, and his succeeding the *Keelergee Bashaw*; and so by course the *Capee Agha*, if he out-live the rest.

PENSION.

† 40 *s. sterl.*

And although all these four eunuchs may wear turbants in the *Seraglio*, and ride (being the chief next the King himself in authority within the *Seraglio*) and are reverenced and respected of all men; yet the three last, *viz. Hazinehdar Bashaw, Keelergee Bashaw,* and *Sarai Agesee,* may not of themselves when they list speak to the *Grand Seignor,* but only answer when any thing is

DIFFERING PRIVILEGES.

asked of them. Howbeit they always attend, with the *Capee Agha*, the person and service of the King, with all the eunuchs under them, and the aforesaid *Aghas*, and *Itchoglans* already spoken of: but these four only govern, and manage the King's houshold affairs; and give order for all things needful and necessary, as well for the days as for the nights provision.

200 EUNUCHS IN
THE *SERAGLIO*.

THEIR GELDING.

All the eunuchs in the *Seraglio* may be in number about two hundred,[3] what with old ones, middle aged, and young ones: they are all of them not only gelt, but have their yards also clean cut off, and are chosen of those *Renegado* youths, which are presented from time to time to the *Grand Seignor*, as aforesaid: few, or none of them, are gelt and cut against their will. For then, as the master workmen in that business do affirm, they would be in great danger of death: wherefore, to get their consent thereto, they promise them fair, and shew unto them the assurance they may have, in time, to become great men; all which must be done when they are very young, at their first coming into the *Seraglio*.[4] For it is a work not be to wrought upon men of years.

THEIR EDUCATION
IN THE FOUR *ODAS*.

They are brought up with the *Itchoglans*, and are instructed in many things as well as they; being removed also from one *Oda* to another; and are last of all taken out by turns of the fourth *Oda*, for to serve the *Grand Seignor* as well as those which are not eunuchs.

IMPLOYMENT.

His Majesty likewise employs some of these his white eunuchs in the government of all the other *Seraglios*, and Seminaries of youth, as well in *Constantinople*,[5] as in *Adrianople*,[5] *Bursia*, and in divers other places: in each of which there are commonly two or three hundred youths, that so by their diligence and care over them, together with the help of other ministers, they may be brought to an excellent discipline; by which they may afterwards prove to be men of good manners and reasonable learning.

And it so falleth out many times, that the *Grand Seignor*, to give way to the other inferior and younger eunuchs, who expect that they shall succeed in order the aforesaid offices, sendeth forth some of the ancient, richest, and of the highest rank, in great imployments, as to be *Bashaws* of *Cairo, Aleppo*, or of some other cities, and provinces in *Asia*, and sometimes *Vizirs* of the bench. For the eunuchs generally prove subjects, though not of great courage, yet of the greatest judgment and fidelity; their minds being set on business, rather than on pleasure.

And for that the eunuchs are more trusty, than any other servants of the *Seraglio*; the *Capee Agha* their patron doth commonly commit such things, as the *Grand Seignor* would have kept for curiosity, unto their custody: who for that end have closets made of purpose to lay up such rarities as are presented to the King; as great pieces of *Amber-Greese* sent from the *Bashaws* of the *Morea, Muske, Treacle, Mithidrate* of *Cairo*,[6] *Terra sigillata*,[7] *Balsam* and other such things of great value; cups also of Agat, Chrystal, and Jasper, *Turkesses*,[8] and other precious stones: all which are so curiously kept, that it seemeth to be admirable. They likewise lay up his *Indian* presents of *Zeva*,[9] and *Civett*; of all which things his Majesty and his *Sultanas* make daily use.

Hard by the eunuchs lodgings in the *Seraglio*, there is a very large place, in which are kept all such goods as fall to the King, as well by them which are put to death, as by those which die of natural diseases; of which the King is master. Now the goods being brought into the said place by the chief *Defterdar*, who receives them from the *Beit il mawlgee*,* and is to bring them thither, the *Grand Seignor* in presence of his chief

THEIR ADVANCEMENT.

FIDELITY.

GOODS OF THE DECEASED.

*An officer which seizeth the estates of the dead, for the King.

servants, having seen and well viewed all, maketh choice of what he thinks fit to reserve, and to give away. The rest is cried in the *Seraglio*, to the end, that if any one there have a will to buy, he may have a good penny worth, and the remainder of that is at last carried into the publick *Bezisten*,*[10] where each parcel is cried up and down, the cryer still naming the most that hath been already offered, and is at length sold to him that bids most; nor may any, that offers a price, go from his word, at least if he be able to perform and stand to it. The money made of the said things is delivered to the *Hazinehdar Bashaw*, and is put into the outward *Hazineh*.

And although the goods did come from out of the houses of such as died, but the day before of the pestilence; the *Turks* nevertheless do willingly buy them, and use them, as if the disease were not infectious at all; affirming that their end is written in their forehead, and that it is a vain thing to think, or seek to prevent it by any human rule, or policy; as either the avoiding the company of infected persons, or the not wearing of the clothes of them that died.

THE *BERSTENZ.*

*A large four square building, where the best and richest wares are bought and sold.

NO FEAR OF PESTILENCE.

CHAPTER VIII

Of the Black Eunuchs, and Blackmoor girls, and women; of the Physicians, and of the King's children.

BLACK EUNUCHS.

THEIR EDUCATION.

KUZLAR AGHA.

THEIR PENSION.

Now as concerning the black eunuchs, and Black-moor wenches which serve the *Sultanas*, and the rest of the King's women;[1] it is to be noted, that the black eunuchs, whilst they are boys, are for the most part kept and taught among the other youths of the *Seraglio*, as the white ones are, until they be come to age, and made fit for service; being taken from thence, they are appointed for the women, and set to serve, and wait with others at the *Sultanas* gate, all under command of the *Kuzlar Agha*, who is their patron, as the *Capee Agha* is master of the white ones, being allowed a pension of fifty or sixty aspars a day, and two vests of silk yearly, with linnen and other necessaries, sufficient for their use, besides divers gifts and gratuities, which they receive from women strangers, [at such times as they let them in to the King's women, and especially from the *Jews* women, who are daily conversant with them. The reason why their pension is so great, in comparison of others, is, that they can never be sent abroad in any imployment, thereby to enrich themselves as the other can; but must for ever stay, and serve in the *Seraglio*.]

They are named by the names of flowers, as *Hia-cynth, Narcissus, Rose, Gillyflower*, and the like. For that, serving the women, and being always near about them, their names may be answerable to their virginity, sweet and undefiled.

The Black-moor girls, are no sooner brought into the *Seraglio* after their arrival at *Constantinople* (for they come by ship from *Cairo*, and thereabouts) but they are carried to the womens lodgings; where they are brought up, and made fit for all services: and by how much the more ugly and deformed they are, by so much the more they are valued and esteemed of by the *Sultanas*. [Wherefore the *Bashaw* of *Cairo*, who for the most part sends them all, is always diligent to get the most ill-favoured, coal-black, and flat-nosed girls, that may be had throughout all *Egypt*, or the countries bordering on it, to send them for presents to the *Grand Seignor*, who bestows them upon his women.]

Now after their coming, if they shall be disliked by reason of some infirmity; then are they sent into the old *Seraglio*, as the white women are, when they are unfit for service, or misbehave themselves: all which is done by the King's order and consent.

The aforesaid black eunuchs, by occasion of being sent with messages to the *Grand Seignor* from the *Sultanas*, may pass through the mens lodgings, to carry little notes to the *Capee Agha* that he may deliver them unto the King; or for to fetch any thing from any of the officers of the *Seraglio*, or to speak with any of their friends at the gate: but otherwise they may not dare to go forth of the *Seraglio* from the *Kuzlar Agha*, without express licence from the *Sultana* Queen.[2]

They likewise are to go to and fro, and to do all other businesses for the *Sultanas* in the womens lodgings: which the white eunuchs cannot perform. For they are not permitted to come there; nor any

NO WHITE MAN MAY
COME AMONGST
THE WOMEN.

THE PHYSICIANS
VISITING THE SICK
WOMEN.

man that is white, but the King only, may see and
come amongst the women; insomuch, as when some
one of them being fallen sick, it is required that the
Hekim Bashaw, who is the King's physician, should
come thither; they must necessarily first have leave of
the King for his entrance, and being admitted to enter
by the *Sultanas* door, he seeth none but the black
eunuchs, all the other women being retired into some
withdrawing rooms, who bring him into the sick
woman's chamber; and she, being closely covered from
head to foot with quilts and blankets, holdeth out her
arm only, so as the doctor may touch her pulse; who,
when he hath given order what shall be done, both for
her diet and medicine, goes his way immediately, by
the same way that he came.

STRANGE NICENESS.

But if she, which is sick, be the Queen or one of
the *Sultanas*, with whom the *Grand Seignor* hath lain,
then her arm and hand, which she holdeth out of the
bed for the physician to feel her pulse, is covered with
a fine piece of white silk or *Taffata* sarcenet, for her
flesh may not be seen nor touched bare; neither may
the doctor say any thing in her hearing, but, being
gone out of the chamber, prescribeth what medicine
he thinks fit: which for the most part, according to
the knowledge and common custom of the *Turks*, is

*Potion, or drink,
or syrup.

PHYSICK MEAN.

but only some kind of loosening and refreshing
*Sherbit,** for they seldom use any other physick; [nor
do I hold their skill sufficient to prepare medicines
for every malady.

But in case the party deceased[3] should have need of
a Chirugeon; she then must do as she may, and suffer
without any scruple. For there is no remedy to conceal
her skin and flesh from him. And as for the other
women, which are not *Sultanas*, or at least which are
not well beloved of the *Grand Seignor*, either for their
person, or for some peculiar and extraordinary virtues:

CURING IN THE OLD
SERAGLIO.

THE KING'S SONS BY
THE QUEEN.

MOTHER'S CARE.

CIRCUMCISION
SOLEMNITY.

HOJAH, OR SCHOOL-
MASTER.

they, needing a chirurgeon, are sent into the old *Seraglio* to be cured, where they shall not want whatsoever may be thought convenient and useful, for restoring them to their former estate.]

The King's sons, which are born unto him by his Queen, are nursed, and brought up together by themselves by choice nurses, which are found abroad without the *Seraglio*. But if his Majesty have sons also by other *Sultanas* (as commonly every *Grand Seignor* hath) then those are brought up a-part, and not with the Queen's; so that every mother careth for her own children, and that with great envy and jealousy: yet they may play together, till they come to be of six or seven years of age; being much made of, sumptuously maintained, and appareled all alike at the King's charge.

They live among the women till they come to be of nine or ten years of age; and, about fourteen, they are circumcised with great pomp and solemnities throughout the whole city, especially the eldest son. For the circumcision of the *Turks* children are like to the Christian weddings; there being used at them great feasting, banqueting, musick, and bringing of presents.

From five years of age until ten, during which time they live amongst the women, they have their *Hojah*, that is, that school-master, appointed them by the King to teach them to write, and read; and to instruct them in good manners, that they may behave themselves decently before the King their father; which *Hojah* comes once a day into the womens *Seraglio*, and is brought into a chamber by the black eunuchs, without ever seeing the King's women at all, whither the children come accompanied with two or three old Black-moor women slaves; and there they are taught for so many hours together, as their tutor is permitted

THE KING'S
DAUGHTERS.

to stay, and then he departeth.

As for the daughters, they are but slightly looked after; nor is the King so tender and careful over them. For as they are not suspected at all, for any thing that may concern the state in future times; [so likewise are they not much respected: yet they are well provided for by the *Grand Seignor* their father, in case they live to be fit for husbands.]

*The word
signifieth a King's
son in the *Persian*
tongue.

THE PRINCE SENT
ABROAD.

After the *Shawh-zawdeh*,* the next heir to the crown, is circumcised; if his father think it unfit to keep him any longer with him at home in the *Seraglio*, he provides all things fitting for to send him abroad; that he may see the world, and learn experience, the better to enable him for to govern the empire after his father's decease; sending along with him one of his principal and trusty eunuchs, for to be his guide and overseer in all his actions; besides many servants to attend upon him: all which he chooseth out of his own *Seraglio*. He allows him likewise sufficient means to maintain him like a prince, as he doth also the rest of his sons, if he have a purpose to send any of them abroad. And so all things being well ordered and prepared for him; having taken his leave of his father and mother (who present him with many gifts, as also the *Sultanas*, and all the *Bashaws*, and great men of the *Port* do) he departs for *Magnesia*,⁴ a city in *Asia*, there to reside in the government of that province; in which he hath not the supreme authority, but governs only as his father's deputy. And should he pass the limits of his commission, he would quickly fall into disgrace, and suspicion of rebellion; as heretofore it hath happened unto divers of his predecessors, sent out in the same manner. Wherefore the eunuch, which is appointed to be his helper and overseer, is bound to give continual advice to the *Grand Seignor* of his deportment, and to the *Vizirs*, of all occurrences

AN EUNUCH IS
OVERSEER.

MAGNESIA, HIS
RESIDENCE.

HIS COMMISSION.

whatsoever, according to the charge given him; and likewise to receive from *Constantinople* such orders and commandments, as are to be obeyed in those parts, where the Prince resideth. So that all things, in a manner, are swayed by the discretion of the eunuch.

CHAPTER IX

Of the cooks, kitchens; diet of the King, Queen, and others; of the manner of Service; of their skullery, and provision of the Seraglio.

The victuals in the *Seraglio*, for the most part, are dressed by *Agiamoglans* brought up to cookery, which are called *Aschees*,* and are known from other *Agiamoglans* by their white caps, yet in the form of a sugar loaf as well as the others are. Howbeit there are belonging to the kitchens, that are therein, more than two hundred under-cooks, and skullions; besides their principal officers, as sewers, caters, and such like: all which are carefully to look to their several kitchens, and not any one to trust another with his business.

The King's kitchen begins to work ordinarily before break of day. For his Highness rising betimes, there must be always somewhat ready for him; because commonly he eateth three or four times a day. He dines usually at ten of the clock in the forenoon, and sups about six at night, as well in the summer as in the winter.

When he hath a will to eat, he tells the *Capee Agha* of it, who forthwith sends an eunuch to give notice of the same to the chief *Sewer*, and he, having caused the meat to be dished up, brings it in dish by dish to the

HIS SITTING AT
MEAT.

King's table; and so his Majesty sits down after the common *Turkish* fashion, with his legs a-cross, having a very rich wrought towel cast before him upon his knees to save his clothes, and another hanging upon his left arm, which he useth for his napkin to wipe his

NOT CARVED.

mouth and fingers. He is not carved unto, as other Princes are, but helps himself; having before him upon a piece of *Bulgar* leather (which is instead of a table cloth) fine white bread, of three or four sorts, well

HIS BREAD.

relished, and always very new, as indeed all *Turks* love their bread best, when it is warm, newly come forth of

NO KNIFE NOR
FORK. TWO
SPOONS.

the oven. He neither useth knife nor fork, but only a wooden spoon, of which there are two always laid before him, the one serving him to eat his pottage,

SYRUPS.

and the other to sup up certain delicate syrrups, made of divers fruits, compounded with the juice of lemmons, and sugar, to quench his thirst. He tasteth of his dishes one by one, and as he hath done with them they are taken off. His meat is so tender, and so delicately dressed, that, as I said before, he needs no knife, but pulls the flesh from the bones very easily with his fingers. He useth no salt at his table, neither

NO SALT, NOR
ANTEPAST.

hath he any *Antepast*; but immediately falls aboard the flesh, and, having well fed, closeth up his stomach

*A Tart.

with a *Bocklava,*[1] or some such thing. And so his dinner, or supper, being ended, he washeth his hands,

BASON AND EWER.

in a bason of gold, with the ewer all set with precious

HIS DIET.

stones.

His Majesty's ordinary diet (as I have been told by some of the *Aschees*) is, half a score roasted pigeons in a dish; two or three geese in a dish; lamb, hens, chickens, mutton, and sometimes wild fowl, but very seldom: and look what he hath roasted for him, so he hath the same quantity boiled, almost of every thing, there being very good sauce for every dish, and other ingredients very pleasing to the palate.[2] He hath

*Little pies.

†It is an *Arabian* word, and signifieth drink: of these *Sherbets* there are very many sorts.

DRINKING ONCE.

NO WORDS AT MEALS, ACCORDING TO THIS SAYING, *EVEL TAZAWM ANDEN KELAWM*: FIRST VICTUALS AND THEN WORDS.

MUTES AND JESTERS.

HIS FAVOUR.

DISHES, AND COVERS OF GOLD.

YELLOW PORCELANE, FOR THE *RAMAZAN*, OR LENT.

likewise broths of all sorts; and divers porcelane dishes full of preserves and syrrups; and some tarts, and *Burecks** after their fashion made of flesh covered with paste:[3] and having made an end of eating, he drinks one draught of *Sherbet*†[4] (seldom or never drinking above once at a meal) which is brought unto him by one of his *Aghas* in a deep porcelane dish covered, standing upon a flat under dish of the same metall.

All the while that he is at table, he very seldom, or never, speaks to any man; albeit there stand before him many *Mutes*, and *Buffons* to make him merry, playing tricks, and sporting one with another *alla Mutescha*,[5] which the King understands very well. For by signs their meaning is easily conceived: and if peradventure he should vouchsafe to speak a word or two, it is to grace some one of his *Aghas* standing by him, whom he highly favoureth; throwing unto him a loaf of bread from his own table: and this is held for a singular grace, and especial favour; and he distributing part of it amongst his companions, they likewise accept of it at the second hand, and account it as a great honour done unto them, in regard it came from their Lord and King.

The dishes for his Highness's table are all of gold, and so likewise are their covers; they are in the custody of the *Keelergee Bashaw*, who attends at the kitchen at dinner, and supper time: and so are all the yellow porcelane dishes, which are very costly, and scarcely to be had for money, in which the *Grand Seignor* eats in the *Ramazan* time, which is their lent, and lasteth a whole moon, and the month itself is so called. Now at that time, the *Turks* never eat in the day, but only in the night; not making any difference at all, in meats; excepting swines flesh and things strangled, of which they are forbidden by their law to eat at any time.

The King seldom eats fish, unless it be when he is abroad, at some garden-house, by the sea-side, with his women; where he may sit, and see it taken himself.

THE REMAINDER OF HIS MEAT.

*Gentlemen waiters.

The meat which remains of that which was at the *Grand Seignor's* table is immediately carried to the *Aghas** table, who wait upon him; so that they, what with that, and their own diet together, are exceeding well provided. Whilst the *Aghas* are eating, the King passeth away the time with his *Mutes* and *Buffons*, not speaking (as I said) at all with his tongue, but only by signs.

HIS SPORTING WITH HIS *BUFFONS*.

And now and then he kicks, and buffeteth them in sport; but forthwith makes them amends, by giving them money. For which purpose his pockets are always furnished, so that they are well contented with that pastime.

THE *CAPEE AGHA'S* DIET.

In the mean time also, the *Capee Agha* eats, in a room a-part, such meat as is prepared for him in his kitchen, being far inferior to the King's diet. And with him do eat the *Hazinehdar Bashaw*, the *Saraj Aghasee*, and sometimes some of the King's physicians, whom he calls in for to bear him company; and such other eunuchs, which are keepers of the *Seraglios* abroad, as do come to visit him. And the remainder of his diet, with a fresh supply from the kitchins, serves *di man' in mano*,† all the other white eunuchs.

†From one to another, or from hand to hand.

In this *interim*, likewise, is meat sent to all the other *Odas*, for the youths there; which is two loaves a piece a day, and a little boiled mutton, with pottage of rice, mingled with butter and honey; which indeed consists more of broth, than substance; it being but thin of rice, and so little flesh in it, that it is well, if it give but a taste thereof, when they sop their bread in the dish.

DIET FOR THE *ODA* YOUTHS.

On the other side, is meat carried in by black

QUEEN AND
SULTANAS DIET.

eunuchs to the Queen, to the *Sultanas*, and to all the other women; wherein is observed the same order, as is aforesaid, with the King: insomuch as, in the space of an hour and half, or two hours at the most, all is dispatched.

QUEEN'S SERVICE
IN COPPER.

The Queen's service is in copper dishes, tinned over; but kept very bright, and clean, and some also of white porcelane: however it is to be understood, that she herself may be served as she pleaseth; and so questionless may all the *Sultanas*, although their ordinary allowance be no other than copper. For

THE KING WITH HIS
WOMEN.

oftentimes the King is amongst them a whole day together, eating, sporting, and sleeping, of which there is no notice taken, nor may any one look into his actions: where, amongst themselves, they make him delicate and sumptuous banquets, over and above the ordinary meals of dinner and supper, of sweet meats, and fruits of all sorts, having daily an abundance presented unto them.

SNOW MIXED WITH
SHERBET.

They drink their sherbet in the summer time, mingled with snow; of which there is a great quantity preserved yearly, for to serve the *Seraglio*; but at a very dear rate. For the snow doth stand the *Port* in more

EIGHT THOUSAND
POUND *STERL.*

than twenty thousand chicquins a year, in gifts, and ceremonies, and other expences at the fetching it in from the hills, and in putting it under ground in houses made of purpose for that use.

COMFETS, AND
CHEESE, NOT USED.

They do not ordinarily use comfets, nor cheese. For the *Turks* do hardly know how to make them, especially cheese, which if they make, yet it never proves good. So that the *Sultanas*, all the *Bashaws*, and other great personages, eat none but Parmesan, of

*Leiger
Ambassador.

which the *Bailo** of *Venice* doth always furnish them, and that very plentifully: for they love it well, and eat heartily of it, when they go abroad upon pleasure, to take the air.

97

ORDER.

For the sundry provisions of the said *Seraglio*, all things are prepared in great abundance; and every particular provision is assigned to particular persons, to take care thereof; so that there is never any want at all of things necessary. [For the officers are sure, upon the least complaint made against them, to lose their places. Wherefore, as it behoves them, they are very careful to see, not only that there be a sufficiency, but also that it be very good.]

BREAD OF THREE SORTS.

The first, and best sort of bread, which indeed is very white and savoury, is for the *Grand Seignor*, the *Sultanas*, the *Bashaws*, and other great ones. The second sort, for them of middle rank. And the third and last sort, which is very black and coarse, is for the *Agiamoglans*, and others of base quality.

MEAL FROM *BURSIA*.

The meal whereof the best sort of bread is made, for the *Grand Seignor*, and the *Sultanas*, is brought from *Bursia*, made of the wheat of that province of *Bithynia*, and growing in the King's own ground. The yearly provision thereof is, about seven or eight thousand keloes, which makes almost so many bushels of our measure in *London*: the which wheat makes the best flour that comes to *Constantinople*; for that is it also ground at *Bursia*, and those mills are far better than any, that are near *Stamboll*.*

QUANTITY.

*Constantinople.

VOLO-WHEAT.

Now for the other wheat, which they spend, it comes, for the most part, from *Volo* in *Græcia* by shipping, where there is a great portion of land belonging to the crown. And a great part of the corn, there growing, is spent yearly in the King's armada, made into bisket at *Negroponte*: some also is sold to the *Raguseans*, and others, who come with their shipping to lade it thence; but they must bring their authority with them from *Constantinople*, underwritten with the chief *Vizir's* own hand. And there is likewise brought yearly to *Stamboll*, of the aforesaid wheat of *Volo*, thirty

QUANTITY.

*Store-houses.

five, or forty thousand *Keeloes*; the which is laid up in magazines,* and is afterwards ground, and most of it spent in the *Seraglio*; that which remains, they sell away into the city.

Nor is it any wonder, that the *Seraglio* consumes so much bread corn. For, besides the ordinary servants, as aforesaid, all the *Sultanas*, and great personages, with divers others, have their daily and due allowance of bread, from the *Keeler*, that is, the *Pantry*, or from his Majesty's bake-house; *scilicet*,[6] every *Sultana* twenty loaves; every *Bashaw* ten; to the *Muftee* eight; and so to divers others a several proportion, even to one loaf a man: all which is ordered, and done by the commandment, and discretion of the chief *Vizir*; their several allowances being set down in the chief *Pantlers* books, or else in his, who is the overseer of the bake-houses; every loaf being as big as three of our penny loaves in *London*, but very light, and spungy, and easy of digestion.

PANTRY
ALLOWANCE.

RICE, AND PULSE
FROM *ALEXANDRIA*.

The rice, and lentiles, and all other sorts of pulse, of which there is a great quantity spent, are brought yearly from *Alexandria* in the Galeons, which make yearly two voyages, and bring out of *Egypt*, not only the said pulse, but also all sorts of spice, and sugar, and a great quantity of preserves, and pickled meats, which the *Turks* much delight in. And as for sugar, there is spent an unspeakable deal of it in the making of *Sherbets* and *Boclavas*,[†] which not only the *Seraglio* useth, but are also ordinary presents, from one *Bashaw* to another, and from one friend to another; insomuch that it is a thing to be admired, that so great a quantity should so suddenly be consumed.

SPICE, SUGAR, AND
SWEET-MEATS.

†Tarts.

LITTLE SPICE
CONSUMED.

True it is, that there is but little spice spent in the *Seraglio*, nor indeed any great store among the *Turks*, [pepper only excepted.] For seeing wine is not an ordinary drink amongst them, they therefore avoid the eating of such things, as do provoke a desire there-unto. Howsoever in the store-houses of the *Port*, there is provision of all sorts of spices, and drugs, whatsoever occasion should happen, that might require the use of them.

EGYPTIAN FRUITS.

There likewise come from *Egypt*, great stores of dates, prunes, and other dried plums, of divers sorts, which the cooks use in their dressing of meat, as well for roast, as boiled in broths: and indeed, they make very delicate dishes of them.

HONEY WHENCE.

*They call them *yoofka*, sig[nifying] flat.

†The *Turks* call them *lokma*, which signifieth, a bit, or mouthful.

‡The *Turks* call it *sakuz Ada*; that is the mastick island, because the mastick grows there.

The honey (of which the *Port* spends a great quantity, both in their broths, boiled meats, pancakes,* frittars,† and coarse sherbets, for the common sort of people) is brought in great earthen jars, from *Walachia*, from *Transylvania*, and *Moldavia*,[7] as well that which is presented by the Princes of those Provinces to the *Grand Seignor*, as that which comes for particular mens accounts. Yet that honey, which is used in the King's own kitchen, come from *Cio*,†[8] and is far better and purer than the other.

OIL WHENCE.

§Governor, next in degree to a *Beglerbegh*.

The oil (of which there is an unspeakable quantity spent, by reason of the many uses they put it unto, as well in their meats, as for their lamps, and the like) is brought from *Modon*, and *Coron* in *Grœcia*; the *Sanjack Beg*§ of that province being bound to see the *Port* sufficiently furnished therewith, from time to time. Howbeit that which is spent in the King's own kitchen, is brought from *Candie* and *Zant*, it being sweeter, clearer, and in every respect better, than that of the *Morea*.

BUTTER FROM *BOGDANIA*, ETC.

¶Boil'd rice.

The butter (of which also there is spent a very great quantity, in that it is used almost in all their meats, especially in that ordinary dish which they call *Pillaw*¶) comes by shipping out of the *Black Sea*, from *Bogdania*, and from *Caffa*, being put into great ox hides, and buffalo hides, with the hairy sides inward; and so

*Store-houses.

QUANTITY.

is laid up in magazines,* for the yearly provisions of the King's court: but commonly they have so much of it, that they are fain to sell part into the city; [as they likewise do by the oil, honey, etc. which are *Beggleek*[9] (that is, for the *Grand Seignor's* own account) when they have more than they think they shall have occasion to spend, and make a wonderful great benefit of it; oftentimes enforcing the shop-keepers to take it at what price they please to rate it at, although it be ill conditioned, and ready to stink.

NO FRESH BUTTER.

LITTLE MILK EATEN.

YOGHURD, SOWRE MILK.

KAYMACK.

The *Turks* are no whit acquainted with fresh butter, there being little, or none at all, made about *Constantinople*; neither do they eat much milk, except it be made sowre, which they call *Yoghurd*. For that, being so turned sowre, it doth quench the thirst: and of that, both they, and the Christians do eat a great quantity in the summer time. They eat also some store of *Kaymack*, that is, clouted, or clodded cream; but that is a dish for the better sort only, it being a meat of too high a price for the vulgar.]

PROVISION OF FLESH.

†So called because the flesh is pressed and made flat.

HOW THEY USE IT.

Now, as for flesh; every year in the autumn, winter drawing nigh, the *Bashaw* causeth the provision of *Basturma*† to be made for the King's kitchens; which must be of cows great with calf. For then (say they) the flesh is most tender and savoury. [They use it in the same manner, as christians use swines flesh. For they make puddings and sausages of it, and the rest they boil and dress after other fashions.

HANGED UP AND DRIED.

This sort of dried flesh (after that it is sufficiently dried and hardened, with hanging a month, or better, in some upper room, and little or no salt used about it, but pressed very flat) will last the whole year following, and eat very savoury. And it is in such great use amongst the *Turks*, and so well liked of, that there is scarce any master of a family, if he be of ability, but doth yearly against winter make his provision of it; and it is held a very thrifty and sparing course. For that then fresh meat would be very dear. But they do not all make their *Basturma* of cows great with calf, (that is for the *Seraglio*) for there are many which love the other better, which is made of oxen and bullocks; and they can buy it far cheaper.

The *Bashaw*, as I said, hath the care and oversight of what is prepared for the King's kitchens, and there are commonly spent four hundred cows every year for the said provision of *Basturma*: there is also fresh beef spent in the *Seraglio*; but the quantity is uncertain.]

The other flesh, which is daily provided, and spent in the kitchens of the *Seraglio*, as I was told by one of the *Aschees*,* is as followeth: sheep two hundred; lambs, or kids when they are in season, one hundred; calves ten; geese fifty; hens two hundred; chickens one hundred; pigeons an hundred pair.[10]

There is very little store of fish spent in the *Seraglio*, either shell-fish or other; yet sometimes the *Aghas* for dainties will eat some. The seas thereabout do exceedingly abound with divers kinds, and they may easily take as many as they please; by reason of which the Christians are plentifully served with fish in the markets, and at reasonable prices, and the common and poorer sort of *Turks* do bear them company in that diet.

The *Grand Seignor*, nor any of his women, or servants in the *Seraglio*, cannot want for fruit, there being at time of year so many presents, of all sorts of fruits, brought thither, besides what comes from the King's own gardens (which are many, and near the city) every morning in great abundance, and excellent good; especially figs, grapes, peaches, and *Caoons*;†[11] the gardeners selling the remainder at a place‡ in *Constantinople*, where only the King's fruit is sold, and bring the money weekly to the *Bustangee Bashaw*, who

400 COWS GREAT WITH CALF SPENT EVERY YEAR.

OTHER FLESH.

*Cooks.

FISH.

FRUITS.

†Melons.

‡Which is called *yemish bazar*, that is, the fruit-market.

afterwards gives it to his Majesty; and it is called *jebbe
akchesee*, that is, the King's pocket-money. For he gives
it away by handfuls, as he sees occasion, to his *Mutes*
and *Buffones*, at such times as they make him sport.
[Now this fruit being sold, the buyers of it do
commonly send it to some great personages; for it is
extraordinary good, and so artificially piled up in
baskets, by the *Bustangees,** that, for the beauty of it, it
oftentimes proves more acceptable than a gift of
greater price.]

The furniture of the kitchens in the *Seraglio*, as
kettles, caldrons, pots, and skillets, etc. are almost all
of brass; and they are so neatly kept, and of such a
largeness, that there cannot be a braver sight of that
nature; insomuch that one would rather think, that
they stood there to be sold, than that they should be
so often used as they are. And as for the dishes, they
are all of copper, tinned over; but so often new
furbished, scowered, and trimmed, that (they being
daily used) it is wonderful to behold their continual
brightness. And of these dishes they have a great
number: but the *Grand Seignor* sustains great loss by
them. For, there being such a multitude of people
served daily from the kitchens, both within and
without, especially upon the four *Divan* days, there are
so many of them stolen, that the *Defterdars*, weighing
the loss and charge of the said dishes, have oftentimes
been almost resolved, to make them all of silver, and
so to consign them to the custody of the *Sewers*, and
Butlers, who should from time to time give account of
them, and look the better to them, and not to suffer
every ordinary fellow to carry away his meat in them,
as they do in the other copper ones: but finding it a
thing so costly, not any *Defterdar*, as yet, hath
performed it, nor adventured to begin, only have
discoursed of it, and approved of that course, as a

WOOD AND FEWEL.

remedy, to prevent their usual pilfering.

The wood, which is spent in the aforesaid kitchens, and in all the *Seraglio*, is an infinite number of weights (for at *Constantinople* the wood is all bought and sold by weight, and so is almost every thing else) there being for the account of the *Seraglio*, which they call *Begleek*, about thirty great *Caramusalls*,*[12] which do nothing else at one time of the year, but sail into the *Black-sea*, there to lade at the King's woods. It is a business, which costeth the *Grand Seignor*, but little or nothing, in respect of the worth of it. [For they have it for the cutting down, and as for the bringing, and unloading of it, it requires little or no charge at all. For the said *Caramusalls* are bound to make so many returns in a year for the King, but receive no freight; and the masters are to see it unladen at the appointed wharf, at their own costs, and charges; receiving only a discharge in the end from the *Stanboll Agha*[†] for that year's service, but no recompence at all. Afterwards they may work for themselves, and go whither they please, till their turns come again for the year following.]

*Ships.

[†] An officer of good account, which taketh care for the city's provision: The word signifieth the Master of *Stanboll*.

CHAPTER X

Of apparel, bedding, sickness, hospitals, inheritance, King's expences, recreations, his going abroad, receiving of petitions; of the King's stables, and Byram solemnities.

THE FASHION OF
THE KING'S
APPAREL.

*A *Shash* is the whole piece (be it long or short) of fine linnen, of which the *Turbant* is made; but the name of the stuff (as we call ours lawn, cambrick, holland, etc. is *Telbent*, whence we falsly call that which a *Turk* wears a Turbant, using the name of the stuff for the thing made up; whereas the true word is *Saruck*, and the *Turks* themselves so call it: it comes from *Sarnach*, which signifieth to wind about, or to swathe.

†Night-attire, for the head.

The *Grand Seignor's* apparel is nothing different in fashion from other mens, saving in the length of his vests, and the richness thereof; nor are his shoes plated with iron at the heels, as other *Turks* wear them, but are raced, and painted like childrens-shoes, with knots and flowers, [or else they are all white. The fashion of his turbant is all one with that of the *Bashaws*; but he wears plumes and brooches[1] in his, and so doth not any *Bashaw* in the Port, except the *Vizir Azem*, and that is upon the day when he makes a solemn shew at his departure for the wars.]

And as for his lodging; he sleeps upon matteresses of velvet, and cloth of gold: in the summer in sheets of *Shash** embroidered with silk, sewn to the quilts, and in the winter betwixt coverlets of *Lusernes*,[2] or of *Sabells*, wearing all night a *Gheje-lick*,† or little *Shash* on his head.

And when he lies alone in his own lodgings, he is always watched by the pages of his chamber, by two and two at a time, changing their watch every three hours; one of them standing at the chamber door, and the other by the bed-side to cover him, in case the cloths should slide off, and to be near hand if his Majesty should want any thing, or be ill at ease. In the same chamber also where he lies, there are always two old women, that wait with burning torches in their hands, which they may not put out, till such time as the King is risen out of his bed. [Now the use of these lights is, for his Majesty to say over his beads, and for to pray by, in case his devotion be stirred up thereto, at midnight, or at *Temcheet namaz*, which is about two hours before day.

TWO TORCH-WOMEN.

WOMENS HABIT.

*Breeches, from the waist down to the heel.

The habit of his women is much like to that of the men. For they wear *Chacksirs*,* and buskins[3] too, and the meaner sort of them, have their shoes shod with iron at the heels.

They likewise sleep as the men do, in their linnen breeches, and quilted waistcoats; having thin and light ones for the summer, and more thick and warm ones for the winter.

NO CLOSE-STOOLS, AMONG THE MEN; BUT THE WOMEN EVER, WHEN THEY GO THE *HAMAN* OR *BAGNO*, CARRY THEM ALONG WITH THEM.

NO PAPER USED AT THE PRIVY.

The *Turks* never have any close-stools, or such like utensils in their chambers; but having necessity they rise, and go to the privies, made in places a-part, where there do always stand pots full of water ready, that they may wash when they have done, for they use no paper in that service, as others do; holding it not only undecent, but an extraordinary absurdity, for a *Mussulman* to put paper to so base a use; seeing that both the name of God, and the *Mahometan* law, are written upon the like. They all put off their turbants when they go about that business; and a *Janizary* may by no means piss with his *Uskuf*†[4] upon his head, but having done, he must kiss it, and so put it on again. For they hold the covering of their heads to be as honourable in a manner, as the head itself.]

†They also call it *Kecheb* that is, a *Janizary's* cap; but *Uskaf* properly signifieth a hood.

STIPENDS, HOW PAID.

The several stipends which the *Grand Seignor* alloweth to those of the *Seraglio*, of what degree or condition soever the persons be, are paid out of the outmost *Hazineh*; and the chief *Defterdar*, who hath a book as well of the names of the stipendiaries, as of their stipends, is bound to send, once in three months, to all the *Odas*, in several bags so much money as their pay comes to, and there they share it amongst them. The like he doth also by the women, and the *Agiamoglans*, paying them in good money. And against the *Byram* which is their *Carneval*, he must send them their vests, their linnen, and such like necessaries; of all which he never fails them. For if he should disappoint them, especially at that time, they would so complain against the said *Defterdar*, [that it would be his utter overthrow; or at the least he should be sure to lose his place; such is the *Grand Seignor*'s care for his servants, that they may not want whatsoever is befitting each particular person in his several degree.]

When any one dies in the *Seraglio*, whether he be *Itchoglan*, or *Agiamoglan*, his chamber-fellows are made his heirs, and that which he leaves behind him is equally divided amongst them and so is it with the young wenches which never lay with the King: but if any great eunuch die, all comes to the *Grand Seignor*. For they are always very rich, by reason of the manifold gifts and gratuities, which daily come to their hands: and if any *Eunuch* of the *Seraglios* abroad, or in other places of government, should die; then two thirds only of his estate fall to the King by *Canon*, the other third part being to be disposed of, according to the *Testator*'s will. This also is only by permission, when the King gives way unto it, and will not, out of his supream authority and power, take all to himself, [as he useth to do by all great rich ones; the King's person being held the principal and most lawful heir

EVERY THREE
MONTHS.

SERAGLIO HEIRS.

EXCEPTION.

of all, they esteeming themselves as slaves, which have received their livelihood, goods, estates, and all that they have enjoyed, meerly from his greatness and bounty; so that they may not grudge to render back again at their deaths, or whensoever he shall require it, all that they do possess. And to this end, there is an officer called the *Beyt il mawlgee*; who so soon as any one dies, or is put to death, makes inquisition after their estates, and so certifies the *Defterdar* thereof, leaving the performance to him, if it be of great import. But the *Beyt il mawlgee*, for his own private gain, doth oftentimes conceal, after search made, a great part of the estate of the deceased; dividing the same privately betwixt the kindred and himself.]

When any ordinary person falls sick in the *Seraglio*, he is immediately carried from his chamber in a cart which is covered with cloth, and drawn with hands, and is put into the aforesaid *Hospital*, or *Lazaretta*[5] belonging to the house only; [where he is look'd unto after the *Turkish* fashion, and kept so closely, that none may come to the speech of him, except the physician, or apothecary, but with great difficulty;] and, growing well again, he must be carried back, in the same manner, to his own chamber where he was at the first.

The expences of the *Seraglio* are very great, as one may gather by what hath been already said: but there are moreover divers other charges of great consideration which the King is at, by reason of the *Sultana* Queen, and then of the chief *Vizirs*; the *Serdars** of his several forces both by sea and land, and the great *Defterdars*, and others; to all which he gives gratuities, according as he seeth fit upon sundry occasions, as well at the times of their going forth, as at their returns from their employments abroad, and upon good services done at home: the which gifts are vests, some unlined, and some lined with very costly furs,

BEYT IL MAWLGEE.

HIS SUBTLETY.

HOSPITAL.

THE KING'S EXPENCES.

*Captains, or generals.

*Daggers.

swords, bows, *Hanjars,** plumes, and brooches, girdles
all set with rich stones, and many other things of
great value; [and again some but of low price,
according to the quality and desert of the parties, to
whom his Majesty is pleased to shew his liberality.]
Nay, the *Hazinehdar Bashaw*, who hath the keeping of
the cloth of gold and silver of *Bursia*, doth affirm that,
in that one commodity, to make vests of, there is

200000 *SULTANAS,*
ABOUT 80000
POUNDS *STER.*

spent yearly two hundred thousand *Sultanas*; besides
what he disburseth for the buying of *Venetian* silks, and
woollen clothes, of which the *Seraglio* consumes a great
quantity, they not wearing, for the most part, any
other.

Neither doth this alone serve the turn. For besides
all this, the *Grand Seignor* gives away all that which is
given him by strangers; and a great part also of that
which comes to him of the spoil of the dead, of which
he is master, as hath been shewed before.

[And surely, should his Majesty want these helps,
he could not long continue his liberality, giving as he
doth, to his women, to his *Bashaws*, and to all such as
are at any time to kiss his hand. Nevertheless, true it
is, that the greatest part of things of value, which he
gives away, in time, come again to his hands. For his

EBBING AND
FLOWING FROM
AND TO THIS
OCEAN.

Sultanas, Bashaws, eunuchs, or other rich men, dying, he
immediately becomes master of all again, or, at least,
of the greatest part of their estate: and so of such
things there is a continual ebbing and flowing in the
Seraglio.

THE QUEEN'S
EXPENCES.

The Queen likewise gives much away. For as she is
presented by many, so is it fit that she should in part
make some compensation; and to that end, she hath an
allowance of vests, and other things in great
abundance. Besides, she hath liberty to dispose of
many of those, which have been worn by the King.]

THE *VIZIR'S* GIFTS.

The *Vizir Azem* is also a giver at the King's charge;

as well whilst he is in *Constantinople*, as when he is upon departure, as general of the *Grand Seignor's* army to the wars: and to that end, before he departeth, he hath brought unto him, from the *Hazinehdar Bashaw*, a great number of vests, and other things; that he may be provided, when he is in the field, with presents, according to the *Turkish* custom; which, in all businesses, and upon every occasion, is, to give and take.[6]

KING'S PAGE.

The King, if he please, may at any time go abroad either by water, or by land: when he goes by water he hath his *Kaik* of sixteen, or eighteen banks,[7] with a very sumptuous and stately poop, covered over with crimson velvet richly embroidered, under which he himself sits, and none but he upon cushions of velvet, and cloth of gold; his *Aghas* standing all on their feet, holding with one hand by the side of the *Kaik*, and only the *Bustangee Bashaw*, who steers the barge, may now and then sit down, that he may handle the helm the better. Now the *Bustangee Bashaw*, by reason the

MUTES HOWLING.

King talks much with him in the *Kaik*, [at which time, lest any one should hear what they say, the *Mutes* fall howling like little dogs] may benefit, or prejudice whom he pleaseth, the *Grand Seignor* being altogether ignorant of divers passages, and apt to believe any information, either with or against any subject whatsoever. His barge is rowed by *Agiamoglans*,[8] which

THEIR MANNER OF ROWING.

are brought up in that exercise; [and indeed they manage the business very well, and nimbly, not sitting at all when they row, but as they fetch their stroke, they step up upon the next bank before them, and so with the stroke fall backward flat on their backs upon the next bank behind them; much resembling the manner of rowing in the gallies.]

HIS GOING OUT BY LAND.

When he goes forth by land, he always rides on horse-back, and goes out, commonly, at the greatest gate, especially at such times as he is to go to the *Moschea,*[9] which is upon the Friday, it being their sabbath, and is accompanied into the city by all the *Bashaws,* and other *Grandees* of the *Port,* besides many of his own houshold servants which go by his stirrup, and his *Aghas* riding after him; having divers *Solacks* also with their bows and arrows, which go before him for his guard. And as he rides along the streets, he salutes the people with nodding his head towards them, who again salute him with loud shouts, and prayers of prosperity and happiness; and for recompence, the King oftentimes puts his hand into his own pocket, and throws whole handfuls of money amongst them. Now they of the *Seraglio,* which go along by his stirrup, have charge to take all such petitions, as are preferred to his Majesty as he rides along either to, or from the *Moschea*: and many poor men, who dare not presume, by reason of their ragged apparel, to approach near unto so majestic a presence, stand afar off with fire upon their heads, holding up their petitions in their hands; the which the *Grand Seignor* seeing, who never despiseth, but rather encourageth the poor, sends immediately to take the *Arzes;** and being returned home into his *Seraglio,* reads them all, and then gives order for redress as he thinks fit. [By reason of which complaints, the King oftentimes takes occasion to execute the fury of his wrath and displeasure,] even upon the most eminent in place, [before they are aware, without taking any course in law against them, only acquainting the *Muftee* with his design, who seldom or never doth oppose him, but causing a sudden execution of what punishments he pleaseth upon them; either putting them to death, or at least turning them out of their places. For as he stiles himself *Awlem penawh,*† so he would have the world to take notice, that such, as

SOLACKS, OR BOW-MEN.

GRATULATIONS, AND GRATIFICATIONS.

PETITIONS PREFERRED.

**Arzes,* or Petitions.

†The world's refuge.

111

lament unto him, shall be sure to have redress and succour from him; although his ministers fail them, or abuse them through their injustice.] Which makes the *Bashaws*, and other great officers, that they care not how seldom the *Grand Seignor* stirs abroad in publick, for fear lest in that manner their unjust proceedings and bad justice should come to his ear. [And indeed they always live in great fear, through the multiplicity of business that passeth through their hands, and in danger of losing their lives at a short warning, as it hath been ever observed, that few *Vizirs* die in their beds, which makes them use this proverb; *that, he that is even the greatest in office, is but a statue of glass.* But, notwithstanding their brittle estate, bribery hath so bewitch'd them, that, hap what will hap, he that will give most shall be sure to speed at their hands.] The *Grand Seignor*, for the use of his houshold, hath in *Constantinople* at a place called *Ahur capsee,** near unto the *Seraglio*, an exceeding large stable of a thousand horses, and upward: and the *Imrohor Bashaw,*[†] which is master of the horse, hath the charge of them, [as of all his other horses, mules, camels, and all his cattle whatsoever, and of all the King's hay and provender; having an under *Imrohor* for his assistant, besides many ordinary grooms, which are to look to them, and see that the *Seises*[‡] keep them in good ease.] Now the said *Imrohor Bashaw*, and his deputy, are to see the *Grand Seignor's* servants provided of horses, at such times as they accompany his Majesty abroad, either solemnly at shews in the city, or abroad at hunting, or otherwise as the King pleaseth.

Besides this stable, he hath divers others in other places, both for his own service, and for the use of his gentlemen, at such times as he, or they shall come thither: namely, at his gardens and houses of pleasure abroad in the country, to which his Majesty useth to

PROVERB.

*That is, the stable wharf; or gate.

THE KING'S GREAT STABLE.

[†]Chief master of the horse: the true word is *Emeer-Ahor*, which signifieth Lord of the stable.

[‡]Horse keepers.

OTHER STABLES.

go very often; but these stables have not above eight, or ten horses a piece in them. [For to those houses he carrieth but few followers with him, and those few are the chiefest *Aghas* of all.]

STALLION HORSES.

He hath also stables of stallions for race in *Bursia*,[10] *Adrianople*, and in divers other places; from which are brought to *Constantinople* very stately colm; besides such as are continually sent him for presents from *Cairo, Damascus, Bagdat*, and other places by the *Bashaws*. He hath also many which fall to his share by the death of great persons: all which are horses of great price, and kept for his own use.

But because there must be a great number of horses, for ordinary services of the baser sort of servants, the King is therefore furnished with low prized nags out of *Walachia*.

HIS NAGS FROM
WALACHIA.

MULES.

Constantinople.

Besides the aforesaid stables of horses, the *Grand Seignor* is provided of five thousand *Mules*,[11] kept near to *Stanboll*,* which serve to carry *Pavillions*, chests, water, and all other necessaries for travel: but because the *Vizir Azem*, at his going out in general, makes use of a great part of them, there is seldom that number compleat at home. And should the King himself go out to the wars in person, his very houshold would use a thousand of them,[12] besides the riding horses. [For the *Ottoman* Emperors are almost as well accommodated in their voyages abroad, as they are at home in the city; and indeed the generality of the *Turks* are so well fitted, against such times as they are to go forth, especially for long journies, as I think no people in the world can go beyond them.]

PUBLICK APPEARING
AT THE *BYRAM.*

The *Grand Seignor* is bound by *Canon* of the empire, upon the first day of the *Byram*, which is their *Carneval*, the *Ramazan* being ended, which is their day-lent, to shew himself publickly, and to let all the great men, and the better sort of his own servants kiss his vest; wherefore upon that day early in the morning, being richly clad, and decked with his best jewels, he cometh forth of his lodgings, at that gate which is kept by white *Eunuchs* in the second court,[13] and sets himself down in a certain place called the *Taht*,*[14] upon a *Persian* carpet of silk and gold, close by the aforesaid gate; and doth not stir thence until such time as all that are appointed have kissed his vest, in token of their reverence and duty towards him; the chief *Vizir* standing close by him, and telling him the names of such as he thinks fit, and their places, to the end the *Grand Seignor* may take the better notice of them. Now to some of the doctors of the law, which are of high degree, the King raiseth himself up a little, to honour and receive them; and to some he shews more grace and affection, than to other some; and indeed to all more than ordinary, especially to the *Muftee*, and the two *Cadeleschers*.

Now this ceremony being ended, he goeth to the *Moschea* of *Sancta Sophia*, accompanied by them all; where having finished the *Namaz*† for that day, he hears a sermon; and at his return, taking his leave of them, he retires himself to his own lodgings, where he dines alone, as he doth upon other days: notwithstanding upon that day he maketh a very sumptuous banquet in the *Divan* for the *Bashaws*, and other *Grandees*, and a very great dinner in the court yard, for all such as did accompany him, and are there present. Then after dinner his Majesty, observing the ordinary custom, sends the *Vizir Azem*, for his *Byramlick*,‡ a very rich vest furred with a costly fur; and doing the like by the other great ones of the *Port* (though with vests of far lower price) he also extends his bounty to all his *Aghas*, bestowing upon them swords, *Hanjars*,§ and such like things; and upon the *Sultanas* costly jewels, *Filjan takeas*,¶ and *Coshacks*‖ all set with stones; besides many gifts to others of the *Seraglio*, giving *Byramlicks*, or, as we say, new-year's gifts, to all.

THREE DAYS
SOLEMNITY.

FIRE WORKS AND
SHEWS.

Every night, during the three days of the *Byram* (for it is but for three days, and so it ends) he causeth shews to be made of fire-works, and such like, by the water-side,[15] which continue until morning, and a great drum is beaten all the while; and that the *Sultanas* may see them, the King comes of purpose into their company to be merry with them, and is more free and familiar than at other times. He also gives free liberty for mirth and sports, both by day, and night, throughout the whole city, during those three days.

There are also invited to these great festivals all the *Sultanas*, which live out of the *Seraglio*, who both give presents to the King, and take *Byramlicks* of him.

PRESENTS TO THE
KING.

FROM THE *BASHAWS*.

FROM THE
SULTANAS.

Moreover in this *Byram*, the *Grand Seignor* is presented by the *Bashaws*, and great personages, with gifts of very great price. For every one strives to exceed another, thinking thereby to win favour. The *Sultanas* also are not behind hand; for they present him with shirts, handkerchiefs, linnen breeches, towels, and such like things of good worth, being all very curiously wrought, the which the *Grand Seignor* afterwards makes use of, for his own wearing.

*Feast.

[The same *Byram** of three days is kept in all his dominions, and throughout the city of *Constantinople*, even in every *Turk's* house; the streets being, almost at every corner, set out and decked with pretty devices,

†Swings.

and *Salunjacks*† of divers sorts, very artificially made, where old and young are solaced; and, giving two or three *aspars* to the keepers of the swings, have sufficient recreation.] But during this feast, it is somewhat troublesome and dangerous for the poor

CHRISTIANS AND
JEWS SCARED.

‡In which time they
drink no strong
drink at all.

Christians, and *Jews*, to walk along the streets. For the *Turks* being then somewhat insolent, and full of wine, putting off the sobriety of the *Ramazan*,‡ do scare them exceedingly; often threatening to mischief them, if they deny them money, when they in that fury demand it of them. And so they do likewise at another *Byram*, which is called the *Coochook Byram*,[16] and comes about three months after the other; in which likewise the *Turks* are wonderful merry, both day and night.

THAT IS, THE LITTLE *BYRAM*.

CHAPTER XI

Of the Old Seraglio, and womens lives therein: of their marriages, and children: slave-selling, and witnesses.

Having oftentimes, by the way, made mention of the *Eskee Saraj,** which is, as it were, a dependant of the King's *Seraglio,* in regard of the use of it; it will not be amiss, briefly to speak somewhat touching the same.

*Old Seraglio.

This is a very large place, immured with a very high wall, surpassing that of the King's *Seraglio*; the buildings are fair; it hath many inhabitants, all women, and eunuchs, and is about three quarters of a mile in compass, being seated in the noblest part of the city.[1] And this was the first *Seraglio*, which *Mahomet* II. built for to dwell in with all his court, when he took *Constantinople*. It hath but one gate belonging unto it, and that is of iron; the which gate is kept and guarded by a company of white eunuchs,[2] and no man may come in thereat, unless it be to bring in such necessaries as they want in the house, at which times they cannot see any of the women.

COMPASS.

BUILT BY
MAHOMET II.

IRON GATE.

Now the women which are therein, are those which are put out of the King's *Seraglio*, viz. such *Sultanas* as have belonged to the deceased *Grand Seignors*; those women likewise, which, through their evil behaviour and conditions, are fallen into disgrace with the King;

WHO ARE THEREIN.

and such as are infirm, or defective in what should belong to women fit for the company and bed of a King; and none else are there, but for some of these causes. All which are governed and look'd unto by an old woman (called also *Kahiya Cadun*) which is made their overseer, and taketh care to see them used according to the custom of the house, every one in her degree; and that they have their diet, and cloathing, with their several stipends in due time; all which is far short of what they had, when they were in the King's *Seraglio*. Howbeit, such, as have been *Sultanas*, live out of the common rank, in their lodgings a-part; and although they are out of the King's sight, and, as it were, out of favour, yet they are reasonably well served.

WOMAN-OVERSEER.

The greatest part of the said *Sultanas*, if they be any thing rich, may, with the *Grand Seignor's* leave, by the old woman's sollicitation, go forth from thence, and marry, and carry with them all that, which they have kept, and stolen. For if they do not carry the business cunningly, at their coming forth of the King's *Seraglio*, if they have aught of any great worth or value, that is known, the *Cadun** takes it from them, and restores it again to the *Grand Seignor*: so that, I say, if they have any thing to bestow themselves withall, they warily make it known abroad, to the end, that some men of quality may become sutors to them, and make them a good jointure.

THEY MAY MARRY WITH THE KING'S LEAVE.

*The mistress of the maids.

In the said *Seraglio*, they have all the commodity of necessaries, that may be, as gardens, fountains, and fair *Bagnos*. And the King[3] himself hath some rooms also therein ready furnished. For sometimes he goes thither to visit his female kindred, as his grandmother,[4] sisters, aunts, etc., who, for some of the aforesaid occasions, have been put out of his *Seraglio*.

CONVENIENCES THEREOF.

The other women of this *Old Seraglio* have but mean allowance; and, had they not somewhat of their own to help sometimes, they would pass but coarsly; so that they are fain to betake themselves to their needles, by which they in part sustain themselves and reap a reasonable benefit. And as in the King's *Seraglio*, the *Sultanas* are permitted to employ divers *Jews*-women about their ordinary occasions; so these women likewise of this *Seraglio* have other *Jews*-women, who daily frequent their companies, and sell their labours for them.

JEWS-WOMEN.

Any *Turk*, be he of the clergy, or of the laity, may, if he please, take seven wives at *Kebin*;[5] but few or none will have more than one, or two at the most, to save charges. Besides[6] he may keep as many *Halayks*,*[7] as he will; and the children, begotten of them, are held as legitimate, as those of the wives; and have as much right to the inheritance of what the father leaves behind him. But between the children of the great ones there is great difference. For a *Bashaw* having married a sister, or daughter of the King, and having sons by them, those sons may not rise above the degree of a *Sanjack Begh*, or a *Capoogee Bashaw*, to the end they may be kept under, being allied to the crown; that so, being but in mean places, they may not be apt to rebel. But their brothers, which their father begat of slaves, may come to be *Bashaws*; for they are free from suspicion, in regard they are not of the blood royal. And hence it is, that those children, which had a *Sultana* to their mother, are so often seen to be in lower degree than the others. For, for the aforesaid reason, he, which is born of the slave, is above him which is born of the *Sultana*: yet with the children of the other subjects it is otherwise; for they all are equals.

SEVEN WIVES.

*Women-slaves.

BASHAWS SONS KEPT UNDER, IF OF ROYAL BLOOD.

DIVORCES.

The parties married may, upon divers occasions

specified in their law, leave one another; especially when they cannot agree, and live peaceably together. And if the man puts away the woman, then he is bound to allow her the jointure, which he promised her, when they were contracted before the *Cadee*, and witnesses: but if the woman forsake the man, then she can recover nothing, but departs only with a small portion, such as she brought with her into her husband's house. And if they have any children, then he must keep the males, and she must take the females along with her.[8] The same order is also observed, and held with married Christians. For, if the husband turns *Turk*, he may take his sons with him, and make them of that profession; but his wife will retain the daughters: and, if she turn *Turk*, she doth the like by her daughters, and leaves the sons to him.

WHAT BECOMES OF THE CHILDREN OF THE DIVORCED.

Now in case a *Turk* take slaves for his use,* he may not sell them again; but they become members of his family, in which they are to remain till they die. But if they prove barren, then they may be sold from hand to hand, as often as it is their fortune.

*To lie withal.

SLAVES SOLD, IF BARREN.

The *Turks* may buy of all sorts of slaves, of every religion, and nation; and may use them as they please (killing only excepted) which the Christians and *Jews* there may not do; for they have liberty only to buy Christians and *Jews*.

There is for this purpose a place in *Constantinople*, near the *Bezisten*, where every wednesday,[9] in the open street, there are bought and sold slaves of all sorts, and every one may freely come to buy for their several uses; some for nurses, some for servants, and some for their lustful appetites. For they, which make use of slaves for their sensuality, cannot be punished by the justice, as they should be, if they were taken with free women, and with *Turkish* women especially.

SLAVES BOUGHT AND SOLD IN THE MARKET.

These slaves are bought and sold, as beasts and

MANNER OF SELLING SLAVES.

cattle are, they being viewed, and reviewed, and felt all about their limbs, and bodies, and their mouths look'd into, as if they were so many horses in *Smithfield*.[10] Then they are examined of what country they are, and what they are good for; either for sewing, spinning, weaving, or the like; buying sometimes the mother with the children, and sometimes the children without the mother, sometimes two or three brothers together, and again sometimes taking the one, and leaving the rest, using no terms of humanity, love, or honesty, but even as the buyer or the seller shall think will best turn them to profit.

Now then there is a virgin that is beautiful and fair, she is held at a high rate, and is sold for far more than any other; and, for security of her virginity, the seller is not only bound to the restitution of the money, if she prove otherwise, to him that bought her, but is for his fraud fined at a great sum of money. And in this *Bezisten* there sitteth an *Emeen*, that is, a customer,[11] who receives custom of the buyers and sellers of slaves, which amounteth to a reasonable sum in a year, for the toll is very great.

RESTITUTION, IF NOT A VIRGIN.

EMEEN.

The *Bashaws*, and other great subjects, though by marriage they become uncles, sons-in-law, or cousins to the *Grand Seignor*, may not, by virtue of their affinity, challenge any more familiarity or freedom with his Majesty, than if there were no such matter of kindred between them; but only presume so far as may well befit their place and dignity; they remaining still slaves, as the others do: nay, their servitude is thereby increased, and they lose a great part of their former liberty. For they must be very obsequious to the *Sultanas*, whom they have married, and turn away the greatest part of their other women, and slaves, if they have any, and must with patience support all their wives imperfections. So that, for this reason, few

NO BENEFIT BY AFFINITY TO THE KING.

LOSS BY IT.

Bashaws of worth, and judgment, seek after such marriages; for they are both chargeable, and bring discontent. But when the King commands, they, as his slaves, must submit and obey, though their vexation and charge increase never so much thereby; and must confess themselves to be highly honoured, and obliged unto his Majesty for so great favour.

RITES OF
MARRIAGE.

The ceremonies of *Turkish* marrying are nothing else, but in the presence of the *Cadee*, who is the justice, to make *Hoget*, that is, a writing expressing the vow, and good liking of the parties to be married; with a specification of the jointure, which the husband is to make to the wife. All which is done in the presence also of witnesses, which are true and honest, without exception. For among *Turks* it is not permitted that

WHO MAY BE
WITNESSES.

every one that will should bear witness; but only such men as are free, of a good age, that can say the *Namaz*,* and have some knowledge in the law, known to be men of civil life and conversation; and, above all, which drink no wine. For the witness of a *Turk*, which drinks wine, is nothing worth, (yet they may drink *Mooselless*,[†12] *Rakee*,[‡13] and *Boza*,[§14] which are stronger than wine) and thus their law commandeth. But for all this, corruption is so crept in amongst them, that now in *Turky*, especially in *Constantinople*, there are (to the outward appearance, grave and honest men) more false witnesses, than in any other part of the world, besides: and who are they, at least the chief of them, but a certain company of beggarly *Emeers*?[15] that is, such as pretend to come of the race and stock of *Mahomet*, always wearing green turbans, by which they are known and reverenced: but they are generally the most ill-favoured men that ever I saw. And with them I may fitly join a great number of poor *Cadees* and *Naibs* out of office, who, as well as the *Emeers*, for money do use that detestable trade, which our knights of the post do

*Common-prayer.

†New wine boiled.

‡*Aquavitae.*

§A drink made of seed, much like new mustard; and is very heady.

EMEERS FALSE
WITNESSES.

*False accusations,
or pretences.

†*Avania.*

TURKS COVETOUS,
AND DANGEROUS.

FORCE OF
EVIDENCE.

practise here with us. And hence it is, that *Avanias** are
so commonly framed; for they can stoutly, and that
with ease, outface the poor Christians and *Jews*; nay
for a bribe they will not spare their own sect, in
bearing false witness; or raising an *Eftera*† against
them. For these *Turks* being naturally given to
covetousness (though they pretend to be lovers of
honesty) and altogether inclined to rapine (yet
without question, there are some honest men amongst
them) when they meet with a fit opportunity, they
will play fast and loose with any man, be he of what
condition soever, for their own benefit. Wherefore it
proves dangerous to have any dealing with them; for
that they with that trick will easily free themselves
from any obligation, or agreement before made;
Judgment there consisting chiefly in the proof by
witnesses; so that a man had need to be wondrous
circumspect and wary, in his proceedings with *Turks*,
especially in matters of contract.

Of their religion, opinions, Clergymen, times, places, and rites sacred; and of the womens small devotion.[1]

THEIR RELIGION.

1. He.
2. *Arab.* God.
3. *Turk.* God.
4. Truth.
5. High Truth.
6. High God.
7. Creator of the world.
8. *Pers.* God.

RESURRECTION.

THE TRUMPET *SOOR.*

SENSUAL PARADISE.

The *Turks* believe in Almighty God, [and give him familiarly these attributes. 1. *Hoo.* 2. *Alloh.* 3. *Tangree.* 4. *Hack.* 5. *Hackteawlaw.* 6. *Allohteawlaw.* 7. *Jehawnee awsoreen.* 8. *Hody,* etc.] And that he is the creator of the whole universe, and will be a gracious pardoner of all good men in the day of judgment. That he is in the highest Heaven, served with especial angels, having from the beginning cast out the disobedient ones, for whom, as also for wicked men, he made hell. And as they affirm everlasting life to be in these two places, *viz.* heaven, and hell; so they confess, and wait for the resurrection of the body to be reunited with the soul, at such times as the fearful trumpet, which they call *Soor,* shall be sounded by *Mahomet,* at the commandment of the great God of the judgment.

They believe also, the life everlasting in *paradise* to be such a happiness, as consists only in delighting and pleasing of the senses, and that they shall have there the use of natural things in all perfection, without making any difference; enjoying perfect health,and free from all manner of trouble and vexation. And on the contrary, that in hell the use of the foresaid things shall be in unquenchable fire, and shall have a most bitter and loathsome taste, and they which come there shall continually be tormented with innumerable vexations, and fearful fights: and this is all that they conceive of heaven, or hell; either for the reward of the righteous, or the punishment of the reprobate.

FATE.

They say moreover, that the power of God is such, that having at the creation of man prefixed, and appointed a set time for his end, it is impossible that the wit or device of mortal man should be able to divert, or prevent it; wherefore in the wars, and in all other occasions, they are so much the more bold, resolute, and courageous; being persuaded that their end is written in their foreheads, and that it is not for them to go about to avoid it, so that if they die, *Emmer Allohung*, it was Gods will it should be so. [Now this their opinion makes them to laugh at and scorn the *Greeks*, who burn waken candles at holy wells, hang rags upon trees, which they rend from the clothing of the sick, and use divers other charms for to drive away diseases.]

THE COMMANDMENT OF GOD.

CHARMS USED BY THE *GREEKS*.

They also affirm God's power to be such, that, after mens bodies are risen again, he will give them such an agility, that they shall be able in a moment to pass from one heaven to another, even to the farthest parts of them; to visit and embrace their wives, mothers, brothers, and others of their kindred; the heavens being all transparent, of diamonds, rubies, and christall.

AGILITY IN THE NEXT LIFE.

TRANSPARENT HEAVENS.

As concerning Gods throne, or seat of Majesty; they affirm, that every one cannot behold it, by reason of the brightness of the beams, which come from his eyes; and by reason of the unspeakable splendor proceeding from his glorious face; so that the angels, and prophets only have the grace to enjoy that sight. [And of the angels they report thus, that they are

GOD'S THRONE.

THE ANGELS.

continually serving, and praising God, and ready to obey his will. But I have read in a book which they call *Ahvawlee keeyawmet*, that is, the state of the day of judgment; written by a famous *Sheyk* amongst them, a most ridiculous discourse of the angel *Gabriel*. For he writes, that *Gabriel* hath a thousand six hundred wings,[2] and that he is hairy from head to foot, of a saffron colour, having in his forehead a sun, and upon every hair a star; and that he dives three hundred and sixty times a day into *Noor dengiz*,* and ever as he riseth out of the water he shakes himself, and of every drop that falls from him there is an angel made, after the likeness of *Gabriel* himself; who until the end of the world do pray unto God, and praise him, upon their beds; and these young angels are called *Roohawneyoon*. Many such discourses there are in that book: but because they are vain, I leave them to the *Turks* that believe them, especially the common sort, who think that whatsoever is written in their tongue must of necessity be true, and that they are bound to believe it.

They hold that in *paradise* there is a tree, which they call *Toobaw*,[3] upon whose leaves are written the names of every living man; so when God's will is that such, or such a one should die, God shakes off his leaf into *Israel's*[†] lap, who looks upon it, and reads it, and having seen what God's pleasure is, he, after the party hath been dead forty days, sends an angel to carry his soul, according as the leaf shall direct him, either into heaven, or hell; for upon his leaf, not only his hour of death is written, but also what shall become of him after he is dead.]

They say, that almighty God sent four *Pegambers*, that is, prophets into the world, to instruct, govern, and save mankind, each of them being holy, pure, and undefiled, *viz.* 1. *Moosaw:* 2. *Dawood:* 3. *Isaw:* and 4 *Muhammed:* and that God sent to every one of them, by

ANGEL *GABRIEL.*

*A sea in paradise.

A TREE IN PARADISE.

[†]This *Israel* they say is an angel.

FOUR PROPHETS, AND FOUR BOOKS.

1. Moses.
2. David.
3. Jesus.
4. Mahomet.

his angel *Gabriel*, a book, that they themselves, being first perfected, might the better know how to instruct the people. To *Moses* he sent the *Tevrat*, that is, the old law; to *David* the *Zebur*, that is, the psalms; to *Jesus* the *Injeel*, that is, the gospel; and to *Mahomet* the *Kurawn*, that is, the *Alcoran*. And that the three first prophets with their people did fail somewhat in the laws given them by God: but *Mahomet* coming last, brought a law, more true, plain, clear, and sincere, in which all such as believe should obtain the love of God. But they say that all other nations continue still in their errors, and, having sucked of their mothers milk, do not embrace the truth. For which obstinacy and blindness, being, by right, deprived of all hope of coming to heaven; they have no other means to recover the same, and to come thither at the day of judgment, but by *Mahomet's* protection, who is the only intercessor and mediator unto almighty God; and standing in the dreadful day of judgement at the gate of *paradise*, he shall be sought unto, and intreated by the other three prophets to save their people also; and his goodness and clemency shall be such, as to make intercession for them; so that the good Christians, and the good *Jews* shall by his means obtain everlasting life, with perpetual fruition of sensual delights, as aforesaid; but in a place a-part, and inferior to the *Turks*, they being beloved of God, and more dear unto him than others.

The women also shall come into heaven, but shall be in a place far inferior to men, and be less glorified.

All the prophets are held in great honour amongst them, and they never name any prophet but they say *Aleyhoo selawm*, that is, health or salvation be upon him.

They call Moses, *Musahib Alloh*[4] that is, a *Talker with God*; and David *Hazrette Dawood*, that is, *venerable David*; and Jesus *Meseeh, Roohullah*, and *Hazrettee Isaw*,[5] that is, *Messias, the Spirit of God*, and *venerable Jesus*; and *Mahomet*,

Resul Allo, that is, the *Messenger of God*.

When they speak of Christ Jesus, they speak very reverently of him, and confess that the *Jews* through envy apprehended him, and falsly, and maliciously condemned him, and led him along to put him to death: but the angels, being sent from God, took him away from them in a cloud, and carried him up into heaven; at which the *Jews* being astonished, and extreamly vexed, took one that was there present, and crucified him in his stead; being unwilling to have it known that Jesus was the Messias, he being in heaven in company of his brethren the prophets, beloved of God, and serving him, as the other prophets do.

These are the main and principal foundations of their religion, upon which they build and frame the course of this their present temporal life; and by which they hope to obtain a life everlasting and happy; affirmed by their prophet to be full of the delights and pleasures of this world, but enjoyed in all perfection and excellency, in a supernatural and incorruptable manner.

The ministry of their religion, or rather their confused sect, is as followeth.

First, they have a *Muftee*,[*6] that is to say, an expounder, or declarer of law cases; who is also amongst them as an archbishop is with us, for he is the *Primate* over the church, and must be a man very expert in the law, and accustomed to do justice, chosen by the *Grand Seignor* himself: the which *Muftee's* charge is, to oversee and hear all such matters of weight, as are belonging to the law, or to the church, in case his inferiors, as *Moolaes*,[†] *Cadees*, etc. should fail in the due performance of what belongs to their several places. And to this end, every Tuesday he must assemble all the chiefest of them which are in town, or at least the greatest part of them, to his own house;

THEIR OPINION OF CHRIST.

*Muftee. This word comes from *Fetha* which signifieth to open in the *Arab.* tongue.

THE *MUFTEE'S* CHARGE.

†*Cadees* of the highest rank, the word signifieth lords.

HIS DISPUTATIAN ON THE TUESDAY.

where he disputeth with them for the space of three or four hours, putting divers cases to them, and taking their answers from them in writing: but by this means he oftentimes entraps many of the *Cadees* which are in office especially such as are given to bribery. For when any plaintiff or defendant is assured, that the *Cadee* which had the cause before him, hath wronged any of them; then the party offended makes his grievance known to the *Muftee*, who against the next Tuesday frames a case, as like unto it as possibly he can, but of another subject, and in other mens names; so when they are come together he wittily puts forth that amongst the rest, and that being resolved with the rest, he looks upon it; then he calls that *Cadee*, which committed the fault, and privately rebukes him for it.

The like course is taken by many, which come to the *Muftee* himself to be resolved in some point of law; lest that the *Muftee* should know either party by naming them, and so lean to what side he pleaseth: but after this manner he cannot easily deceive them.

It is derived from Muftee.

The *Muftee's* chief imployment is, to answer all such propositions as are made unto him; upon cases of conscience, and the rites of the *Turkish* law. The which answers are in few words, very brief, and they are called *Fetfaes*,*[7] that is, declarations or judgments of the *Muftee*; with which he may compel, not only the *Cadees* and *Bashaws* to the performance of the contents thereof; but the King's own person is also bound to see them executed, and to stand to his decree. For they seek altogether to amplify this sect of lawyers, in honour of their prophet the law-maker; and the *Muftee's* authority is so much the more regarded, for that he is upheld very stoutly by the whole order of the *Cadees*.

HIS POWER.

HIS REVENUE.

The *Muftee* hath his revenue a-part in land of about six thousand *Sultanas* a year; but being put out of his place, leaving the revenue to his successor, he hath then but a thousand aspars a day, as the *Cadeeleschers* have when they are in office: howbeit their uncertainties amount always to a far greater matter.

And although this *Muftee* hath not an absolute rule and command over the *Muftees* of other parts of the King's dominions; yet by his policy he ever prevails with the *Grand Seignor*, and effecteth whatsoever he undertakes, especially when he hath the *Vizir Azem* to his friend, who in degree, dignity, and authority is his superior.

CADEELESCHERS.

Next to the *Muftee*, there are two *Cadeeleschers*, that is to say, *Judges* of the armies, one of *Græcia*, and the other of *Natolia*; who also being men of the law, and they which always succeed the *Muftee*, have the oversight of all the other *Cadees*, and the placing or the displacing of them is in their power; which *Cadees* are justices, and there is one in every city and town, to do justice, and end controversies between man and man, and to punish offenders; but they are changed every three years, and others put into their places, by the *Cadeeleschers*, with order from the *Grand Seignor*: which selling of *Cadeelicks** is an unspeakable benefit to the said two *Cadeeleschers*.

*Cadees places.

CADEES, AND THEIR ORDERS.

†Lords.

Amongst these *Cadees*, they have also their orders, *viz.* those of the first rank, and they are called *Moolaes*,[†] which are always imployed in the chiefest cities; the other are but *Cadees*, and they get employment as they can, by their good and upright carriage in their places; a third sort there is also of this kind, which are called *Naibs*, and they serve in small towns and villages, as deputies to the former, but in time come to be as high as they. Now the *Cadeeleschers* keep each of them a book, wherein are exactly set down the revenues of every particular *Cadeelick*[‡] both in *Græcia*, and in *Natolia*, so that, by their books they know the better how to

NAIBS.

BOOKS.

‡*Cadees place.*

furnish any place that is void, and at what rates to sell them; none of them being worth, or yielding above five hundred aspars the day, gratuities and bribes excepted.

This order of *Turks* only, amongst the rest, hath this large privilege, which is, that they may not be put to death as other *Turks* are: so that, if any of them by committing some notorious villainy, or offence against the law, should deserve death, it must then be done, by an express and absolute command from the *Grand Seignor*, and that very warily and secretly; but this happeneth very seldom, or never.

The *Muftee* and other *Cadeleeschers* are changed at the King's pleasure, for there is no office among the *Turks* during life: howbeit their ordinary continuance is three years; their chief fortune depending wholly in the obtaining the grace and favour of the chief *Vizir*.

All the aforesaid men of the law, *viz.* the *Muftee*, the *Cadeeleschers*, *Moolaes* and *Cadees*, wear their *Turbants* far bigger than any other *Turks*, and made up after another fashion, in token that they ought to be reverenced above others; and although their habit be in fashion very like other mens, yet in this there is great difference, which is, that their wearing is commonly chamblet,[8] and the finest cloth, but no silk, or cloth of gold at all.

Then, next to these orders, they have a governor of the *Moscheas*, called the *Moteevelee*;* whose chief imployment is to look after the revenues of the church, and after the repairing of the great *Moscheas*: then *Sheihs* which are high priests, and *Eemawms*, which are parish priests; and next to them, *Muyezins*, which are as our church-clerks; all which are imployed in the service of the church, both in praying, preaching, calling the people to prayer, burying the dead, reading upon the graves of the dead, and to conclude all such offices as

READERS.

*Cathedral church.

†This word is
derived from *Ders*,
which signifieth a
lesson.

PRAYERS FIVE
TIMES A DAY.

UPON FRIDAY
SIX TIMES.

‡Clerks.

MANNER OF
CALLING TO
PRAYER.

§The words which
the *Muyezin* useth to
say in the steeple.

CLEANNESS AND
PURIFYING.

¶Unclean.

are any way belonging to the church, for the edifying of the people.

And in every *jawm** there are *Mudeereeses*† which are readers, that teach scholars the common prayers, and instruct them in the service, and duties, belonging to the church, being paid for their pains out of the revenues of the *Moscheas*.

They pray five times a day ordinarily (as well in the *Moscheas*, as in their private houses, or wheresoever they are) *viz.* about four of the clock in the morning, which they call *Sabawh Namaz*, or *Temcheet Namaz*: at noon, and that they call *Oileh Namaz*: between three and four o'clock after noon, which they call *Ekinde Namaz*: between seven and eight at night, and that they call *Acksham Namaz*: and at midnight, which they call *Ghejeh Namaz*; and upon the Friday (which is their sabbath) six times: for they pray then at nine of the clock in the forenoon also, and that is called *Selaw*. Now upon that day there are more *Muyezins*† which cry in the *Meenares*, or steeples, than upon other days; for at all those hours instead of bells, the people are called to prayer by the voice of one or two of them standing in the steeples, or turrets, which are of a reasonable height, and join to the *Moscheas*; by whose voices, and repetition of the *Aazawn*,§ they are stirred up to the praise of God, and *Mahomet*, and so they prepare themselves for prayer.

The condition of them which are to pray, is only to be corporally clean; it being altogether unlawful for any *Turk* to enter into the *Moscheas*, with an intent to pray, if he find that he hath any natural pollution, or carnal uncleanness about him, be it of what condition soever, or of never so small moment. Wherefore, for their cleansing, every one is bound either to wash himself in the *Bagno*, if it be for carnal commerce, until which time he remains *jenoob*,¶[19] or for other sorts of uncleanness, or small offences, with cold water; every place and city abounding with *Bagnoes*, both publick and private; and every church-yard with very fair fountains for the use of the common sort of people; so that every one must do his *Awb dest** before he pray.

Now, immediately after every one is cleansed, and come into the church, the *Eemawm*† begins with a loud voice to pray, sitting before all the company with his face towards the south east;‡ and the people, being placed in orderly ranks with their faces the same way, do altogether imitate him in gesture. For of themselves a great part of them would not else know how to perform that business, scarcely one in twenty understanding what the *Eemawm* says. For they pray in an unknown tongue as well as the Papists do: and their prayers consist chiefly in rising up, falling down, kissing the ground, and sometimes sitting still; one while touching their eyes, sometimes their faces, then stroking their beards, and anon their heads; again sometimes looking over the left shoulder, and sometimes over the right; saying some few words in the praise of God, and *Mahomet*: the churches being all matted underfoot, and in some places there are carpets spread for the better sort of people.

The said prayers, according to the hours of prayer, are divers, some longer, and some shorter; none of them being above an hour long, only the prayer in the evening of the *Ramazan*, which is longer than the other prayers.

They pray, as I said, after the *Eemawm*, who is their guide, and is much esteemed of, if he have a good voice, as we esteem of our singing men.

They also use preaching upon every *Jumaa ghun*§ in the *Ramazan*: and when they will pray for any good success in their wars, or curse any *Jelawlee*,¶[10] they then

PROCESSION, AND CURSING.

have a custom to go a procession along the streets by two and two, but without any lights, or any such things in their hands; and as they go along, they praise the name of God, and read very long prayers, which they have for those purposes, the people still crying Amen at the end of every prayer; and then they hold that rebel, or enemy, whosoever he be, to be without all doubt accursed, and themselves prosperous in their enterprizes.

OTHER CONVOCATIONS AND PRAYERS.

In the times of trouble and affliction, they publish in the most eminent places a convocation of all the chief men, and ecclesiastical persons in the city; and of the common people also such as will come may, to pray in the fields which are for that use, therein imitating the *Jews*; and being all come together, divers of their *Santons**[11] (esteemed for their shew of holiness) make sermons of exhortation to fortitude, patience, and to the love and fear of God. But if those troubles continue still, they then use the prayers of forty hours, and of forty days, for they are so call'd, in the chiefest *Moscheas* built by the Emperors; which prayers are said by a company of church-men, who are belonging to the said *Moscheas*; and if all fail, then they all fall to sacrificing; for that is held to be of greatest force to put away evil, and the best thanksgiving for benefits received.

*Holy men.

SERMONS.

SACRIFICING.

RAMAZAN CEREMONIES.

All the ceremonies, which they use in the *Ramazan*, are no other, but to abstain from eating and drinking in the day time. For they have leave to eat all the night long, if they will (that is, from the *Acksham Namaz*, which is about seven or eight o'clock at night, until the *Sabaw-namaz*, which is about four o'clock in the morning) and what they please, without any difference of meats. And at twilight they light lamps round about the steeples, which burn till morning; the *Eemawm* of every parish taking special notice who is

LAMPS.

PRIEST.

often wanting from church, especially in the evening, and who drinks wine, or eats in the day time. For besides that they should be held despisers of the law, they should be most severely punished, if they were found in any such fault.

EXAMPLE OF
SEVERITY.

I remember, that *Nasooh Bashaw* being *Vizir Azem*, and riding through the streets in the *Ramazan*, espied a *Turk* that was drunk with wine; so, forthwith he caused him to be brought unto him, and without giving him any respite, for the recovery of his lost wits, caused a ladleful of boiling lead to be poured down his throat, wherewith the wretch perished immediately.[12]

SACRIFICES.

The *Grand Seignor* useth in the *Ramazan*, as well as in the times of troubles and afflictions, and so do the *Bashaws* and other great men, to sacrifice divers sorts of beasts, both at the sepulchres of such as have been held for holy, and valiant men, and at the *Moscheas* too. Now some do it privately; but the Kings have still commanded, that their sacrifices be done publickly, and in the open streets, and at the gates of the city, dividing the flesh of the beasts among the people: yet some part of it is sent to the *Bashaws* themselves, and to the other grandees of the *Port*. These sacrifices are used very often; for by that means they think to appease Gods wrath, and regain his love and favour.

*Puritans.

BEADS.

Those *Turks* which seem to be professors of religion and devotion, and would be accounted *Sofees*,* do commonly read, as they walk along the streets, and have their beads longer than other men, carrying them in their hands into the *Moscheas*, and are ever busy with them as they walk up and down the streets, that the world may take notice of their feigned zeal: but they pass, or rather poste them over very quickly; for whereas the Papists say the *Pater noster*, or an *Ave Maria*;

1. God is pure.
2. God defend.
3. God is great.

they say only two words; as for example, 1. *Subhawn Allah*, or 2. *Istighfir Allah*, and sometimes 3. *Alloho ekber*.

PILGRIMAGE.
MECCA TEMPLE.

Many of them go to *Mecca*, and to *Jerusalem* on pilgrimage. To *Mecca* to visit the temple which they say was built by *Abraham*, in which *Mahomet* in the time of idolatry did hide himself; of whom they affirm, that, when he was almost forty years of age, he received the Alcoran from God by the hand of the angel *Gabriel*, and that from that time the *Mussulmanlick* began, that is, the true belief; and shortly after he died, and his sepulchre is visited by all such, as go to the said

JERUSALEM.

pilgrimage. And when they go to *Jerusalem*, they go not to visit Christ's sepulchre; for they say, he did not die: but they go to see the places, which he most frequented, as being a miraculous prophet, who raised the dead to life, healed the sick, gave sight to the blind, and wrought many such wonders, which never any prophet could do but he. They go likewise to the

VALLEY OF
JEHOSHAPHAT.

valley of *Jehoshaphat*; for they say, that in that place shall be the resurrection at the day of judgment. Now all such as have gone the said pilgrimage, and return

PILGRIMS.

home again to their houses, are ever after called *Hagees*, that is, pilgrims, and are very much reverenced and esteemed of all men. There are also divers *Turks*, who, forsaking the world, leave all that they have, and go to live near to the foresaid valley, for devotion; and to be nearer to the place of resurrection, supposing thereby to get a great advantage to themselves, above the rest at that day.

Many there be likewise, which profess a kind of living, out of the common course and custom of the world, being clothed wonderful poorly and raggedly, with white felt caps on their heads, that beg for their living, and lie in the courts of the *Moscheas*, and in such like places; and these are accounted very holy men; for they pray much in the view of the world, and live always, in outward appearance, in the love of honesty; preaching this doctrine to the standers by, that it is impossible perfectly to arrive unto, and gain the love of God, but by the ladder of human love, and innocency; and for this cause they betake themselves to that course of life, that they may be in charity with all the world, and be accepted of God, and rewarded for it in heaven; under which colour of holiness they live at ease, and deceive the world, every one being bountiful unto them. For the poor, simple, and ignorant people do daily throng about them, receiving their benedictions, for which they give them money. They go many times up and down the city, from house to house, singing certain prayers for the prosperity of the family; and seldom, or never, go away empty.[13]

Besides them, there are also some, who, like hermits, live in rocks, and on the sides of mountains, and in other solitary places, neglecting the world, conceiving that course of life to excel all other for innocency and holiness; to whom also many men and women do resort, and give money for their prayers and benedictions.

CIRCUMCISION.

The greatest ceremony, for pomp and solemnity, which is used amongst the *Turks*, is that of circumcising their children, wherein they greatly differ from the *Jews* in this one particular. For the *Turks* never circumcise them, till they be past ten years of age, following the example of *Ishmael*, whom they imitate; alledging that *Abraham* loved him, and not *Isaac*, and that it was *Ishmael* whom *Abraham* would have sacrificed.

THE LOCK OF HAIR.

Until the very day of circumcision, they let a lock of hair grow on the crown of the head, as long as may be, but afterwrds they cut it shorter: and the reason why they must let it grow is, only to shew that they are not as yet circumcised; until which time they are not accounted perfect *Mussulmen*,* nor may till then pray in the congregation. They wear the lock broided,

*True believers.

and plaited, and hanging down the middle of their back, over their uppermost coat, that every one may see it. This circumcision is done without the church, because of the shedding of blood; all the kindred and friends being invited unto it, in token of joy and gladness. They use the like ceremony with those, which turn from any other religion, and become *Turks*; who, in token that they embrace the religion of *Mahomet*, do, before they are circumcised, hold up their forefinger, and say these words, *Law illawho illaw Allha ve Muhammed resul Allah*, that is, There is no God, but God alone, and *Mahomet* is the messenger of God.

There are in the cities, and by the highways also, in most places of the *Grand Seignor's* dominions, for the benefit both of the inhabitants and travellers, divers *Hawns*,*[14] commonly called *Canes*, in which wayfaring men do lodge, and refresh themselves and their horses. There are also hospitals in cities, and colleges for the bringing up of youth, where they may learn to read and write; every *Moschea* built by the Emperors, and all other great *Moscheas* having large revenues, out of which, by the will of the founders, the said colleges and hospitals are maintained. For the Emperors, by canon, should not build any churches, but in memory of some notable conquest, or memorable enterprise, by which the church may be provided for: nor *Sultanas* neither may build, unless it be the Queen-mother to that Emperor who reigns at that time when she goes about it. For the building of which they are at infinite charge, dedicating them with great solemnities for the said victory, be it what it will be. When an Emperor builds a *Moschea*, and that it is almost finished, and the main *Cubilo*[15] or round roof is to be laid on; to cap or crown as it were the whole fabrick, then are invited all the *Bashaws*, and other great men, to come to the solemnity, but every one of them doth send, the day

*Canes.

HOSPITALS AND COLLEGES.

LIMITED.

A CEREMONY AT THE FINISHING A *MOSCHEA*.

139

before, his present of vests of cloth of gold, velvet, sattin, etc. all which being that day hanged upon cords, on the outside of the top of the church, the *Grand Seignor* himself comes thither, and, being set under his pavillion in the church-yard, all the chiefest of them, to whom he also giveth vests, kiss his hand one after another. This being ended, the *Muftee* makes a prayer, and then the *Cubilo* is put on, and this is their consecration;[16] the said vests, which were hanged up, being afterwards shared amongst the master workmen.

The same ceremony is also used among the *Turks* in building of their houses, at the closing up the roof. For they invite their friends, who either send them vests, or handkerchiefs, and hang them up after the said manner, which also fall to the workmens share; the guests are feasted for their pains, and that is the warming of the house, as we call it in England.

MOSCHEAS.

MAGNIFICENCE.

In these *Moscheas* there are some very costly pieces of work, and exceeding well set forth and proportioned; as well for the largeness and neatness of those places where the people pray; as also for the beautiful porches, galleries, and large paved courts, which compass the said *Moscheas*; adorned with very stately pillars, and fountains built all of curious marble, besides their colleges and hospitals near unto them; to which, as I said, belong very large revenues, insomuch that some of those *Moscheas* may be compared with the richest churches in the world. They are built all of wonderful fair stone, with their *Cubiloes* covered all over with lead; the pillars within the churches being either of *Porphiry*[17] or some such costly stones, and the basis thereof all whited. Now the pillars in time of prayer shine most gloriously, by reason of the abundance of lamps that are burning: the which lamps are curiously fastened into round iron hoops, in

LAMPS.

compass as big as the hoop of a butt; upon which there are divers rounds of lamps one above another, and are let down by copper chains from the roof of the church: in every *Moschea* there are three or four such circles of lamps, or more, according to the bigness of the church.

There are no benches in the *Moscheas*, nor any thing to sit upon; only a little place raised from the ground for the priest, and another right over against it, but somewhat lower, for the *Grand Seignor*, at such times as he comes to prayer;[18] all the rest sitting upon the ground, as ordinarily they use to sit in other places: wherefore the pavements, although they are of very bright and clean stone, are covered with very fine mats of *Cairo*, which are kept wondrously neatly. For besides the *Grand Seignor* no man may come into the church with his shoes on; but must leave them at the door, or else give them to their servants to keep.

When any one is dangerously sick, and in their judgments past hope of recovery; then they send for the *Imawm*,* who comes, and useth comfortable speeches unto him, and prayeth by him; and, the party dying, they wash him all over with water; then having wound him up in his *Kefen*, or winding-sheet, and laid him in a coffin with his face downward, they carry him to his grave with his head foremost. Now if the party that is dead be a man, or a man-child, then they set a turbant upon the coffin; and if it be a woman or a girl, then they set a *Filjan Takya* upon the coffin, for distinction sake; that is, such a cap as the women wear, with a brooche and feather in it. Again, if the party be a virgin, they oftentimes, provided they be people of quality, set garlands and boughs of oranges upon the coffin. They are accompanied to the grave by the churchmen, and their own kindred, and many strangers also, which pass by, willingly go along with

NO SEATS.

MATS.

SICKNESS.

*Priest.

MANNER OF BURYING.

GARLANDS AND BOUGHS OF ORANGES.

WOMEN GO NOT
TO BURIALS.

NO LIGHTS.

*Clerks.

TOMBS OF THE
EMPERORS.

them, (for they hold it a very meritorious work to see the dead well buried) but no women at all; (yet women may afterwards both weep and pray upon their graves) nor do they carry any lights in their hands, or censors, or howl and cry after them as the *Greeks* do; but the *Muyezins** sing all along as they go, calling upon the name of God, and their prophet *Mahomet*, and praying for the health of the soul departed: and at their return there is some kind of coarse banquet made for the company for their pains.

The tombs of the Emperors most commonly are built upon the ground, close by their graves, and on each grave there stands an empty coffin, covered either with extraordinary fine cloth, or else with velvet; having turbants set upon them of the fashion of those which the Emperors themselves did wear, with brooches and sprigs of feathers in them: and there stand great candlesticks both at the head, and at the feet of the said graves, and two lamps burning continually day, and night. Now these tombs are for the most part built in little chappels close by, but not adjoining to the *Moscheas* of the said Emperors. There is no great store of workmanship about any of their tombs. For they are of the fashion of a chest, about seven foot long and about two foot and half broad; but either side is cut out with flowers, gilded over, and at each end an *epitaph*. Now in these chappels there are *Muyezins*, and *Derveeshes*, who by turns continually read in the Alcoran, and pray with their beads, for the glory of the Emperors deceased. The *Vizirs, Bashaws,* and other great men also, imitating the Emperors, do the like, but with less pomp, and charge: and they which have no burying place, near the *Moscheas*, may make them near their dwelling houses, and be buried there, or if they please in any other part of the city, provided that the ground whereon they build their tombs be

COMMON TOMBS.

their own. The common sort are carried out of the city, and buried in the fields, which serve only for that purpose; having one stone set upright at the one end of their grave, and another at the other end, for a token that one hath been buried there: (for by the law, howsoever it is not strictly observed, they ought not to bury where one hath been buried before) upon which is graven the name, degree, and country, or any thing else that they please of the parties deceased. Besides, if it be the tomb of a man of quality, they usually set a turbant cut out in marble upon the head of it; or if a woman, then a cap of marble, such as the women wear.

*Colleges.

†Holy men, professing innocency.

Among the *Turks* there are no religious houses, or monasteries, unless the *Teckebs** of the *Meulevees*,[19] which are an order of *Derveeshes*,† that turn round with musick in their divine service.[20] The *Turks* generally are bred up to arms, and very few can write, or read. Nay, it hath been sometimes seen that a *Bashaw Vizir* of the *Port*, which had not his education in the King's *Seraglio*, hath sat to do justice in the *Divan*, and hath not known either to write, or read, but hath been enforced of necessity to learn to write a few words of course, for the signing of commandments, bills, warrants, and the like. And among the *Turks*, he that can but read, and write, is held a very learned man, and esteemed far above others, by the common ignorant people; insomuch that when a crafty fellow hath got a book, which he knows will please their humours (they altogether delighting in books like *Palmerin d'Oliva*, the knight of the fun, *Amadis de Gaule*, and the like) he forthwith gets him with his book to some *Cahve*

‡Houses where they drink *Cahve*.

house,‡ or other, where there is always great resort, and there, being set down in the middle of them, he falls to reading, the people evermore giving credit to whatsoever he says; and so having spent an hour, or two, he takes their benevolences, which is usually more than the price of his book comes to; such is their simplicity, and such is their delight in hearing a man read fables.

WOMENS RELIGION.

As for the women, there is no heed taken, or reckoning made of their religion at all; therefore I speak of it last, but for modesty sake, I must conceal what the *Turks* are not ashamed sometimes to judge of them. For they never go to church, so that if they happily have a will to pray at the hours of prayer, they do it in their own houses, using the same preparations as the men do.[21] Nevertheless their honesty, and good carriage is much looked after; the *Imawms** of every parish being bound to hearken diligently after their deportment; who, if they discover any thing that is amiss, must reveal it to their husbands, that they may put them away if they will; or else to their fathers, or kindred, if they be unmarried, that they may take some course for to reform them.

WOMEN GO NOT TO CHURCH.

*Priests.

And although the women may not be conversant with any other men, than with their husbands, fathers, or brothers; and although they live in lodgings a-part, by themselves, out of the sight of men, and go always abroad with their faces covered; yet many of them, being extraordinarily wanton, are very dishonest and lascivious, who taking the opportunity of their husbands absence, at the wars, or in some long journey, under colour of going to the *Bagnos*, and being covered withall, go whither, and to whom they lust, knowing that the worst of it is to be put away, if so be it should at any time be discovered.

Notes

by
Godfrey Goodwin

Introduction

1. Thomas Dallam, *Early Voyages and Travels in the Levant* (Hakluyt Society, London, 1893).
2. Although the house later became a tavern, the façade survived until the end of the nineteenth century when it was finally pulled down. As one of the most splendid examples of a great merchant's town house, the façade was given to the Victoria and Albert Museum, where it can still be seen in the court that serves as the museum shop.
3. Vice-Admiral Sir Adolphus Slade, *Records of Travels in Turkey . . . in the Years 1829, 1830 and 1831*, 2 vols (London, 1833).
4. N.M. Penzer, *The Harem* (London, 1936), p. 37.
5. D. Gjertsen, *The Newton Handbook* (London, n.d.), p. 241.
6. Ibid.
7. G.A. Menavino, *Trattato de Costumi, et Vita de Turchi* (Florence, 1548, 1551, 1560).
8. A. de La Motraye, *Travels in Europe, Asia, and in Parts of Africa*, 3 vols (London, 1723–32).
9. Unpublished manuscript in the Manuscript Room of the British Museum: Harl. MSS., 3408.

Letter from John Greaves to George Tooke, Esq.

1. Indeed it was.
2. The book had already been commissioned twenty-five years previously with minor omissions and differences of detail (see the Introduction to the present book).

CHAPTER I

1. Seraglio, Saray or palace. It was then known as Yenisaray (New Palace) but is now known as Topkapısaray (Gun Gate Palace), which was, strictly speaking, only the summer palace at Sarayburnu (Seraglio Point) rebuilt about 1818 by Mahmut II (1809–39).

2. The Bab-ül-Hümayün (Gate of Majesty), built by the Conqueror, Fatih Mehmet II (1444–46; 1451–81), and embellished with marble in the nineteenth century. In Bon's time there was a great saloon built above it where the harem ladies could watch the comings and goings.

3. See the Glossary for the correct modern Turkish spelling, together with an English translation, of the Turkish terms used by Withers.

4. The Arz Odasi (Hall of Petitions or Throne Room) was restored after a fire later in the seventeenth century.

5. This room is little bigger than its water closet.

6. There were many kinds of turban according to the wearer's rank and office. During Bon's period the sultan's turban was large.

7. Dining-rooms as such did not exist. A large round tray of food set on four short legs transformed any room, including the Divan Hall, into a dining-room.

8. The *hamam* (Turkish bath) had a hall for disrobing, a tepid room and a hot room. *Hamams* were centres of social life, especially for women incarcerated in a harem.

9. These rooms were often in the vaults which supported the harem and royal quarters, in particular because the land fell precipitously towards the Golden Horn.

10. The Enderun Kolej ('College Within'), or Palace School, for pages and the school for princes above the quarters of the Chief Black Eunuch.

11. The main pool was built under the rooms of Murat III (1574–95) in the sixteenth century. There the sultan could watch his girls disport themselves in water heated by an immense (extant) boiler. It is possible that the pages were allowed to use this pool on Thursdays.

12. These games took place in the open ground between the palace and the Sea of Marmara now occupied by the military and by tourist coaches.

13. The Bab-ül-Hümayün (Gate of Majesty).

14. Only for the pages. They greatly enjoyed the freedom and the wine that was used as medicine. All women were confined to the large harem hospital below their dormitory area.

15. This is ironic: the 'great hall' was in fact the church named Haghia Irene, which means Holy Peace. It was the sister church to Haghia Sophia, or Holy Wisdom. Both are matchless examples of Byzantine architecture.

16. The Orta Kapı, or Middle Gate.

17. Later, a small private kitchen was established in the Third Court at the back of the harem.

18. For Queen read Valide Sultan (Queen Mother).

19. The senior officer of the household who had a large staff to feed.

20. The main stables were below the sports ground by the Sea of Marmara. A great many mounts had to be sent to graze in the suburbs.

21. The Bab-ül-Sa'adet (Gate of Felicity) through which only the sultan could ride, and before which the portable gold throne would be set on state occasions.

22. This additional paragraph appears in the 1625 version.

23. It was very shallow.

24. An extra line from Bon, 1625, reads, 'I looked also through a window which was in the wall of the said Hall.'

25. Ceramic tiles from Iznik and Kütahya. Some were of the finest known. In the anteroom to Murat III's chamber, for example, there is an arcade with a stylized prunus behind to represent a garden.

26. Bursa was famous for its fruit and vegetable gardens and for its weaving. Its silk fabrics rivalled those of Venice.

27. We have suddenly returned to the Second Court. The writer clearly was not sure where he was going.

28. What was considered most carefully was a building's relationship to the ceremonial functions and symbolism of the Saray.

CHAPTER II

1. The Vezir Azam was Grand as opposed to Chief Vizier—the office conferred on Süleyman the Magnificent's (1520–66) intimate childhood friend, Ibrahim Pasha, in 1524.

2. I.e. the whole of Ottoman Europe, including Albania, Bosnia, Bulgaria, Greece, parts of Hungary, Serbia, etc.

3. But only with the concurrence of the Şeyhülislam (Grand Mufti).

4. Servers.

5. The common folk were not above stealing the dish from which they had eaten as a souvenir.

6. As with Byzantine etiquette, crossed hands demonstrated that they held no weapon.

7. The *hattı hümayun*, or royal edict, could be very elaborate if the petition was of great importance.

8. Two hours in the 1625 version.

9. The officers of the janissary corps held ranks related to the kitchen and symbols of cooking utensils were worn on state occasions (see *Churbagee* and *Churva* in the Glossary).

CHAPTER III

1. Probably meaning Gate. The custom of Muslim rulers to dispense justice from the palace gate is used symbolically. The Porte came to mean the gate to the Grand Vizier's offices and palace.

2. Another precaution against assassination.

3. A sash rather than a sleeve in order to protect the ruler's hand.

4. Dragoman, or interpreter.

5. It was one way of asserting the greatness of the monarch whom the ambassador represented.
6. Kaftan: the great coat of velvet or silk brocaded in the Venetian manner.
7. Canon laws were made by the ruler and his government in addition to Holy Writ or the laws of the Koran.

CHAPTER IV

1. The correct term is *kul*. This is not a slave in the sense of a galley-slave. All the household, janissaries, pages at the Palace School and girls in the harem were *kul*: that is, members of the sultan's family, bound absolutely to him and unable to question his commands. They were nevertheless treated with respect and were formally freed after a number of years. The women in the harem had servants who were indeed slaves. They were usually black and were undoubtedly seen as inferior until they too were manumitted.
2. These figures are grossly exaggerated. Even a sultan as besotted as Ibrahim I (1640–48) did not achieve that number. At the other extreme, Süleyman the Magnificent was so in love with Hasseki Hürrem (Roxelane) that after their marriage the harem dwindled into a remnant of old maids. Bon exaggerates still further: he estimates 3,000 women in all—they must have been strap-hangers.
3. Imported by Jewish traders. Many were brought and Circassian parents reared their daughters for the harem, selling them at a high price.
4. These horsemen raided villages as frequently as country squires in Europe went hunting fox or deer.
5. Meaning converted to Islam like the boys of the Christian levy: and it was Holy Writ that no Muslim could be made a slave.
6. She had much more power than a housekeeper.
7. Only the new recruits.
8. Strictly, *kamara* meant a ship's cabin or the House of Lords or the House of Commons, deriving from Latin. Here it is used to mean dormitories. On rising, the recruits stowed away their bedding and the divans became sofas. A tray was all that was needed to turn the former dormitory into a dining-room.
9. A myth. Bon's informant no doubt spoke from hearsay.
10. She was known as the First Kadın (First Lady) until the boy became sultan, when she became Valide Sultan (Queen Mother). But the Western use of the word 'queen' is merely convenience. Neither the Valide, who ruled the harem, nor any other woman could be a queen or exercise the sovereignty that the title implies. She was 'sultan' only in the sense that the royal daughters were—in other words, a princess—and not even Hasseki Hürrem could hope to be more.
11. First Kadın.
12. *Kebin* is not explained by Withers because it derives from Persian although the word was used in Turkey. It means the bride price.
13. Mosques, not churches.
14. These were mainly situated down the Bosphorus or at the Sweet Waters of Europe at the head of the Golden Horn. The palaces tended to be small since only a few chosen courtiers were invited to attend the sultan.

15. Some princesses were married many times because their husbands fell from favour and were executed. Marriage was intended to bind a powerful subject to the sultan but it in no way bound the master to the subject.

16. On these occasions, there were grand ceremonial processions, both of the presents from the groom and of the princess's dowry. These were exclusive of the landed estates with which the sultan invested the princess.

17. The aspar was the silver coin on which all salaries were based.

18. The sequin was known as a crown and was worth 9s 6d in the pre-decimalized British coinage, in other words about 50p. Today it would be worth £20 or more.

19. This gossip has appealed to the ingenuous for centuries. If it happened at all, it was rarely, since it was totally alien to Islamic law.

CHAPTER V

1. Cadets. They did not really become pages until their last year.

2. At the most.

3. The children were recruited from all over the Balkans, including Bosnia, and also included prisoners of war. The Albanians were reputed to be the fiercest fighters.

4. A child can hardly be a renegade.

5. The boys could be older when there was a shortage of recruits.

6. Salonika and Smyrna (Izmir) were the chief entrepôts for cloth, some of which was bought at Genoa; it was an important part of the London export trade.

7. Usually at Edirne before reaching Istanbul if they were recruited in Europe.

8. Including the use of the science of phrenology.

9. *Oturakcı* means a retired janissary. Pensioners were permitted to remain in their barracks if they chose and there inspire or bore new recruits with stories of their heroism.

10. No mention is made of Balkan boys being sent to farms in Anatolia in order to learn Turkish and build their physique. Such recruits could not expect to reach either the Saray or the lesser colleges.

11. Therefore he has the sultan's ear and so becomes a confidant.

12. This contradicts other accounts: although the recruits were allowed out on duty, it is unlikely that they were free to go where they pleased.

13. Although *kiler* means pantry, the food probably came straight from the kitchen.

14. *Halvet Hümayun* literally means Royal Privacy but it is best translated as 'The King comes!' as happened in royal gardens in Europe. The call is not recorded in Bon.

15. Bon states never fewer than 500.

CHAPTER VI

1. The *içoğlans* became pages to the sultan and were known as sons within the Saray.

2. And also shows that they were unarmed.

3. Certainly exaggerated. If the youth were stupid it would not be sensible to keep him.

4. Since the pages did not usually go out and have a chance to spend money, this pocket money, which was paid quarterly, was saved against their future marriage.

5. Withers has transposed passages from Bon remarkably liberally throughout the last five paragraphs.

6. Archery required a long apprenticeship since it was all too easy to lose the bow finger.

7. Another exaggeration. It would have been wasteful of good military material.

8. But there are references to unnatural practices in washrooms. Youths and men confined during their most virile years were unlikely to be saints.

9. Only white eunuchs were tutors in the Palace School.

10. 'Lewdness' in place of 'filthy actions' in the 1625 version. Bon wrote 'vizj' from *viziare*, to corrupt.

11. Except as a hobby with some sultans.

12. Bon says up to a limit of 40 aspars a day.

13. A future page had to wait for a place because there could only be 39 of them in the sultan's entourage. The sultan himself made up the 40th place with its magic and mystical significance which was taken seriously: Murat II (1421–44; 1446–51) first abdicated in his 40th year, for this was advocated in *The Council for Princes* specially edited for him. Forty was the Turkish for infinity.

14. Withers' list more or less agrees with Bon's (but his spelling is more capricious). However, whereas Bon lists the chief gatekeeper (as *cameriere maggiore*, meaning valet or groom) and the chief pastrycook, Withers lists the Master of the Bath and the chief huntsman. Obviously, Withers deliberately corrected Bon's list because he believed his version to be the more accurate. However, there were 39 *içoğlans* of the Fourth Chamber, therefore leaving room for yet more appointments which could have varied from period to period. Considering the strictness of Ottoman court etiquette, this is not a convincing explanation of the discrepancies.

15. Russian leather.

CHAPTER VII

1. Mutes were frequently employed at courts in Europe (like that of the Gonzagas at Mantua) throughout the Renaissance.

2. Bon states that it was 10.

3. Usually fewer; and in the beginning, under Mehmet II, 24.

4. Unlike the white eunuchs, the black were operated on in monasteries in Egypt before being sent for sale in Istanbul.

5. Now Edirne.

6. An electuary used as an antidote to poison.

7. Making a deep orange or red pigment. *Terra sigillata* is Lemnian earth for making seals.

8. Turquoise.

9. Hyssop. *Zufah* (Urdu) or *Zufah-Yabis* (Hindi). Costly, it was often adulterated

with lavender or rosemary oils but presumably not in the Saray. Used generally for perfume and flavouring, in the Saray it was more likely to be used against troubled stomachs, as advocated in islamic medicinals. Too much was harmful. John Gerard, the herbalist, also advocated its use. The question is why it was imported when it grew in the Middle East and Europe. However, Bon merely calls both ziva and civitt fine cloth from India on a par with silk or damask. The Italian word is *tela*, or a spider's web.

10. The 1625 edition compares it to London's Royal Exchange.

CHAPTER VIII

1. Withers omits Bon's reference to pashas and other dignitaries in Egypt presenting these boys and girls as gifts to the sultan.
2. Meaning Valide Sultan. Strictly speaking, her rank was that of princess.
3. I.e. diseased.
4. Now Manisa. Traces of the vast terraced nursery gardens which produced literally tons of tulips and other bulbs for Topkapısaray can be seen on the hillside.

CHAPTER IX

1. *Baklava* is the dessert of the Middle East. It consists of puff pastry filled with nuts and traditionally dripping with honey—nowadays replaced by syrup, which is oversweet and lacks the tang and 101 choices of flavour offered by good honeys.
2. Peter the Great ate far more, starting with dozens of eggs before breakfast.
3. Today, *böreks* are also made with cheese, spinach and other fillings. They can be triangular, or big flat crusted flans or rolled into cigar shapes with minced lamb: the last being considered the best.
4. Pure fresh fruit juice, iced with snow in summer.
5. Deaf and dumb language.
6. Allowing.
7. And from Trabzon, which still produces delectable honey.
8. A misprint for Candia (the modern Kandia on Crete; the Turkish name is Girid).
9. *Beylik* means a noble estate, but here is used in the sense of crown property.
10. Bon states: 4 calves, 50 geese, 100 hens.
11. Melons. Bon only praises the royal fruit in general. It is Withers, because of gastronomic enthusiasm, who specifies the varieties.
12. Karamürsel is also the name of the Turkish naval base on the Gulf of Izmit.

CHAPTER X

1. Egrets' feathers in jewelled clasps.
2. Fur of lynx or martens.
3. The buskins were attached to the *çakşırs* unlike the baggier *shalvars* (*şalvar*).
4. The felt hat of the janissaries was very stiff and folded over at the back to hang between the shoulders. This is emblematic of the sleeve of Haci Bektaş, the

dervish saint who founded a popular order.

5. Note that Withers does not translate the Italian into Quarantine Station.

6. Also between themselves. Generosity is an endearing Turkish trait.

7. Twelve to fifteen banks according to Bon.

8. More often by the *bostancı*, or Corps of Gardeners.

9. Copied from Bon's Italian. *Cami* (mosque) in Turkish.

10. There are still racing stables outside Bursa.

11. Bon states 3,000.

12. Bon states 10,000: a more probable number.

13. Bab-ül-Sa'adet.

14. This is the mobile throne, which was easily dismantled. It is now on display in the Treasury Section of the Saray, which was originally the Pavilion of Mehmet II. The throne is plated with gold and studded with emeralds and other gems.

15. There was an extensive summer harem at Sarayburnu (Seraglio Point), between the Golden Horn and the Sea of Marmara.

16. Also known as Şeker Bayram (Sugar Holiday), a feast especially enjoyed by children.

CHAPTER XI

1. The grounds had been much larger until 1549, when Süleyman the Magnificent gave half of it to form the esplanade that carries his religious foundation with its great mosque.

2. Surprisingly: one would expect them to be black.

3. That is, Ahmet I (1603–17).

4. The grandmother was the Venetian Safiye Valide who, as Bon states, had long dominated the empire under her loving husband Murat III and her son Mehmet III (1595–1603).

5. Bon correctly states that Islamic law only permitted four wives whatever the *kebin* (bride price) offered.

6. These paragraphs have been reorganized by Withers.

7. These were usually Georgian, Armenian or Circassian girls.

8. This is a correct and succinct explanation of marriage and other laws, for example, which gives Bon's report its aura of authenticity.

9. It was open on other days too, but Christians could only visit on one of them and they could not purchase a slave.

10. The major meat market of the City of London.

11. In the sense of customs officer.

12. Molasses: in Turkey, boiled grape juice of little alcoholic strength known as *pekmez*. Şeker (sugar) *pekmez* is molasses and was not used for drinking except in distilled form which made, in effect, a coarse brandy forbidden to the Muslim community.

13. *Raki* is a grain spirit flavoured with aniseed or wormwood. It is common in Mediterranean countries, where it is known as *arak, oozu, absynthe*, etc.

14. *Boza* is a mildly alcoholic beverage made of fermented millet. A winter drink,

it is peddled hot from house to house as a nightcap. A few *boza* houses remain and serve nothing else. It is nowhere near as strong as wine nowadays.

15. Emirs—not nobles—in an ironic sense. Genuine Seyyids claim descent from the family of the Prophet: there are not many such.

CHAPTER XII

1. This chapter has been reorganized by Withers.
2. All religions have their lunatics and no educated Muslim would have taken the 1,600 wings of Gabriel seriously.
3. The Tuba is said to have its roots in the sky.
4. *Musahib Allah* (more precisely, means Companion of God).
5. *Hazret Isaw* (most excellent Jesus).
6. The Grand Mufti, or Şeyhülislam, was the first and foremost of the judges of the *ulema*.
7. A *fetva* is an opinion given by the mufti on a point of law rather than a judgment. These *fetvas*, which were often ambiguous, were essential before a sultan could be deposed and strangled, for example.
8. Cambric. In a miniature in the *Süleymanname*, the 'men of the law' are shown wearing robes and trains of a light blue watered angora as opposed to the red silk worn by cardinals.
9. *Cenub* means south but here it is confused with *cenabet* (a state of ritual impurity or exclusion).
10. *Celah* were disbanded soldiers without land or pay, together with dispossessed villagers and failed students, among other discontents, who pillaged unguarded villages and travellers in the first quarter of the seventeenth century.
11. *Santons* were dervishes, or members of one of the various Sufi sects, or mystics.
12. It is hard to believe that even a Grand Vezir as vile as Nasuh Pasha had boiling lead quite so readily available. Nasuh was appointed several years after Bon had left Istanbul but while Withers was still there.
13. The equivalent of Christian friars, with some of the same virtues and some of the same vices.
14. *Hans* (khans or inns) had cells at first-floor level over storerooms round a courtyard. This courtyard was defended by a great door that was locked and bolted at night.
15. Cupola.
16. The equivalent of the British 'topping out' ceremony—the celebrations of the building workers and architects when a building is finished.
17. Only a small percentage of the columns are of porphyry. Marmara (Proconessian) marble proliferates and there are many examples of verd-antique, Egyptian granite and other re-used Byzantine materials.
18. The *hunkar mahfile* is the private gallery or lattice-walled room set in the south-east corner of a mosque next to and higher than the mihrab and having a mihrab of its own. It is usually much higher than the platform for the muezzin. The setting apart of the caliph and sultan arose from the assassination of the early

caliphs and the consequent need to protect them.

19. The Bektashi and other dervish orders also have their own *tekkes*.

20. Symbolizing the movement of the spheres.

21. In the sixteenth century, special galleries were built for women, who, presumably, had previously prayed at the back of mosques for the sake of decency.

Glossary

WITHERS' SPELLING	CURRENT TURKISH SPELLING	ENGLISH TRANSLATION
Aazawn	*Adhan*	ritual call to prayer
Acksham Namaz	*Akşam Namaz*	evening prayer
Agha	*Ağa*	*agha* (the *agha* of the janissaries was their captain-general)
Agiamoglan	*Acemioğlan*	janissary recruit
Ahur capsee	*Ahur kapısı*	Stable Gate
Ahvawlee keeyawmet	*Ahvalli kıyamet*	the state of the world's end
Aleyhoo selawm	*Aleykümselâm*	peace be with you
Allo; Alloh	*Allah*	God
Alloho ekber	*Allah akbar*	God is Great
Allohteawlaw	*Allah illallah*	God is God: there is only one God
Arz	*Arz*	petition
Aschee	*Aşçı*	cook
Avania	—	demand for repayment of a loan
Awb dest	*Abdest*	ritual washing of hands, feet and face before prayer

Glossary

WITHERS' SPELLING	CURRENT TURKISH SPELLING	ENGLISH TRANSLATION
Awlem penawh	Alem penah	Protector of the World; the sultan
Bashaw	Paşa	pasha
Basturma	Pastırma	dried salt meat
Begleek; Beggleek	Beylik	royal estates, leased to senior officers for life; province
Beglerbeg	Beylerbey	governor; viceroy
Beit il mawlgee; Beyt il mawlgee	Beyt ül-Malcı	Lord Treasurer
Berber Bashaw	Berberbaşı	chief barber
Bezisten	Bedesten	market hall
Boclava; Bocklava	Baklava	baklava (sweet pastry)
Boza	Boza	beverage made of fermented millet
Bugdania	Boğdan	Moldavia
Bulook Bashaw	Bölükbaşı	cavalry officer; manager
Bureck	Börek	puff pastry
Bursia	Bursa	Bursa
Bustangee Bashaw	Bostancıbaşı	head gardener; commander of the sultan's guards (he was also Master of the Household, Captain of the Royal Barge and chief executioner)
Byram	Bayram	religious holiday
Byramlick	Bayramlık	festival gift, or new clothes for a festival
Cadee	Kadı	judge or magistrate

Glossary

WITHERS' SPELLING	CURRENT TURKISH SPELLING	ENGLISH TRANSLATION
Cadeelick	*Kadılıkı*	area of jurisdiction
Cadelescher; Cadeelescher; Cadilescher	*Kadıasker*	chief justice of Rum (meaning Europe, from the word 'Roman') or Anatolia; strictly, a military justice
Cadun	*Kadın*	mother of a prince; lady of rank
Cahve	*Kahve*	coffee
Caimekam	*Kaymakam*	chief of police
Caoon	*Kavun*	melon
Capee Agha	*Kapı Ağa*	Captain of the Gate
Capoochee	*Kapıcı*	gatekeeper
Capoochee Bashaw	*Kapıcıbaşı*	captain of guards
Caramusall	*Karamusal; Karamürsel*	merchantman
Chakshirs; Chacksirs	*Çakşır*	trousers with leather boots attached
Cheshneghir Bashaw	*Çeşnigirbaşı*	Master of the Commissariat (*çeşnigir* = tasting for poison)
Chiaush	*Çavuş*	doorkeeper or messenger
Chiaush Bashaw	*Çavuşbası*	head doorkeeper or messenger
Chiohadar Agha	*Çokadar Ağa*	head valet (*çokadar* = waterproof)
Churbagee; Churbegee	*Çorbaci*	senior officer of janissaries (a rank akin to colonel)
Churva	*Çorba*	soup or broth of many kinds
Coochook Byram	*Küçük Bayram*	'Little Bayram' (*küçük* = little) [see *Byram* above]
Coshack	*Kuşak*	broad belt

WITHERS' SPELLING	CURRENT TURKISH SPELLING	ENGLISH TRANSLATION
Dawood	Daud	David
Defterdar	*Defterdar*	Keeper of the Account Books; minister of finance
Derveesh	*Derviş*	member of mystical sect; dervish
Divan	*Divan*	meeting of the Council of State
Dogangee Bashaw	*Doğancıbaşa*	chief falconer
Eemawm; Imawm	*Imam*	leader of prayer
Eftera	*Iftira*	slander or fabrication
Ekinde Namaz	*Ikindi Namaz*	afternoon prayer
Emeen	*Emin*	controller; customs officer
Emeer	*Emir; Seyyid*	Commander of the Faithful; religious élite descended from the family of the Prophet
Emmer Allohung	*Emir Allahın*	will of God
Eskee Saraj	Eski Saray	Old Palace
Fetfa	*Fetva*	decision or opinion on a legal problem
Filjan takea; Filjan Takya	*Fincan takke*	skull-cap
Gheje-lick	*Gecelik*	nightcap (the head-covering, not the drink)
Ghejeh Namaz	*Gece Namaz*	evening prayer
Hack	*Hak*	God

WITHERS' SPELLING	CURRENT TURKISH SPELLING	ENGLISH TRANSLATION
Hackteawlaw	*Haktaalâ*	God most high
Hagee	*Hacı*	pilgrim to Mecca
Halayk	*Halayık*	female servant or slave
Hamawmgee Bashaw	*Hamamcıbaşa*	royal bath attendant
Hanjar	*Hançer*	dagger
Hattee-humawyoon	*Hattı hümayun*	royal edict
Hawn	*Han*	khan; inn
Hawoz	*Havuz*	pool (of water)
Hazineh	*Hazine*	public treasury (for the receipt of taxes, etc)
Hazinehdar Bashaw	*Hazinebaşa*	royal treasurer
Hazrette; *Hazrettee*	*Hazret*	Excellency
Hekim Bashaw	*Hekimbacı*	royal physician
Hody	*Huda*	God
Hoget	*Hareket*	deed (i.e. legal document)
Hojah	*Hoca*	teacher; chaplain
Hoo: see *Hody*		
Hoonkeawr	*Hünkar*	royal
Imawm: see *Eeemawm*		
Imrohor Bashaw	*Imirahorbaşı*	Master of the Horse
Injeel	*Incil*	Gospel
Isaw	*İsa*	Jesus
Istighfir Allah	*Istiğfar Allah*	to ask pardon of God

WITHERS' SPELLING	CURRENT TURKISH SPELLING	ENGLISH TRANSLATION
Itchoglan	*İçoğlan*	cadet of the Palace School
Janizary	*Yeniçeri*	janissary
Jawm	*Cami*	mosque
Jebbe akchesee	*Ceb harclığı*	pocket money (for harem girls, *acemioğlans*, etc)
Jehawnee awsoreen	*Cihan Asılın*	the Birth of the World
Jelawlee	*Celalı*	rebels; mutineers
Jereet	*Cerid*	(the sport of) javelin throwing while on horseback
Jumaa ghun	*Cuma gün*	Friday
Kahiyah	*Kahya*	deputy to the *agha* of the janissaries and intendant of the Palace School
Kahiya Cadun; Kahiyah Cadun	*Kahya Kadın*	housekeeper; Mistress of the Household
Kaik	*Kayık*	boat
Kamaradoes	*Kamara*	dormitory
Kaymack	*Kaymak*	thick cream; buffalo cream
Kebin	*Kebin*	bride price
Keeler	*Kiler*	pantry
Keelerge Bashaw; Keelergee Bashaw	*Kilercibaşı*	chief butler or pantryman; Master of the Sultan's Wardrobe
Kefen	*Kefen*	winding-sheet
Kemhasir Agha	*Çamaşır Ağa*	Master of the Laundry (*çamaşır* =laundry)
Kurawn; Alcoran	*Kuran*	Koran

Withers' Spelling	Current Turkish Spelling	English Translation
Kuzlar Agha	*Kızlar Ağa*	Chief Black Eunuch
Law illawheh illaw Allawh, Muhammed resoul Allawh; *Law illawho illaw Allha ve Muhammed resul Allah*	*La'ilah illa Allah ve Muhammed resul Allah*	There is but one God and Mohammed is his Prophet
Lezez	*Leziz*	delight
Maazold	*Mazul*	dismissed
Masar	*Masarif*	expenses
Mataragee Agha	*Mataracı Ağa*	cupbearer (literally: Page of the Water)
Meenare	*Minare*	minaret
Meseeh	*Mesih*	Messiah
Meulevee	Mevlevi	Mevlevi (dervish sect)
Moola	*Molla*	mullah; doctor of Islamic law
Moosaw	Musa	Moses
Moteevelee	*Mütevelli*	trustee of pious foundation
Mudeerees	*Müderris*	professor
Muftee	—	senior judge
Muhasabegee Bashaw	*Muhasebeci*	chief accountant
Musahib	*Musahib*	gentleman-in-waiting; aide-de-camp
Mutaferraka	*Müteferrika*	cavalry officer
Muyezin	*Müezzin*	muezzin

Glossary

WITHERS' SPELLING	CURRENT TURKISH SPELLING	ENGLISH TRANSLATION
Naib	Naib	judge (strictly, a deputy or substitute judge, regent, etc, or someone acting for others)
Namaz	Namaz	ritual prayer
Natolia	Anadolu	Anatolia
Nishawngee	Nişanci	Lord Privy Seal
Noor dengiz	Nur Deniz	Heavenly Sea of the Universe
Oda	Oda	room; barracks; dormitory
Oda Bashaw	Odabaşı	captain of the barrack-room
Oileh Namaz	Öğle Namaz	noon prayer
Otoorack	Oturakcı	retired janissary (*otur* = to sit down)
Pawdishawh	Padişah	sovereign; sultan
Pegamber	Peygamber	the Prophet Mohammed
Pillaw	Pilâv	pilaf
Rakee	Rakı	a spirit made from grain
Ramazan	Ramazan	Ramadan
Rechiubtar Agha	Rikabdar Ağa	Yeoman of the Stirrup
Reiskitawb	Reisülküttab	Chancellor
Rejedg	Receb	seventh month of the Muslim year
Reshen	Resim	due; tax

Glossary

WITHERS' SPELLING	CURRENT TURKISH SPELLING	ENGLISH TRANSLATION
Resoul Allawh; Resul Allah; Resul Allo	Resul Allah	Messenger of God
Roohullah	Ruhullah	Holy Spirit
Roohawneyoon	Ruhanı	angel
Sabaw-namaz; Sabawh Namaz	Sabah Namaz	morning prayer
Salunjuck	Salıncak	swings
Sanjack Beg; Sanjack Begh	Sancak Bey	governor
Sarai; Saraj	Saray	palace
Sarai Agasee; Sarai Agesee; Saraj Aghasee	Saray Ağası	Warden of the Palace
Seis	Seyis	groom
Serdar	Serdar	commander-in-chief (strictly, a rank conferred for the duration of one campaign only)
Shash	Şams iş	damask
Shaw-zawdeh	Şehzade	prince
Sheih; Sheyk	Şeyh	sheikh
Sherbet; sherbit	Şerbet	sherbet
Silihtar Agha	Silahdar Ağa	royal sword-bearer
Sofee	Sufi	Sufi (mystic)
Solack	Solak	royal guard (sol = left-handed)
Soor	Sorugünü	Doomsday
Spahee	Sipahi	cavalryman

Glossary

WITHERS' SPELLING	CURRENT TURKISH SPELLING	ENGLISH TRANSLATION
Spaheeler Aghajee	*Sipahi Ağası*	commander of the *sipahis*
Stamboll; Stanboll	İstanbul	Istanbul; Konstantiniyye
Stanboll Agha	*İstanbul Ağası*	commander of thirty-four companies of janissaries
Subhawn Allah	*Sübhan Allah*	Glory be to God
Sultana	—	before name, or by itself, means prince; after means princess; never means queen (in modern Turkish, *Sultana* means princess)
Taht	*Taht*	(mobile) throne
Tangree	*Tanrı*	God
Teckeb	*Tekke*	dervish convent
Telbentar Agha	—	turban-bearer
Temcheet Namaz	*Temcid Namaz*	dawn call to prayer
Teskeregee Bashaw	*Tezkerecibaşı*	royal secretary
Tevrat	*Tevrat*	the 'old law' (i.e. the Pentateuch)
Toobaw	*Tuba*	Tuba (a tree in paradise)
Turnackgee Bashaw	*Turnacıbaşı*	Royal Nail-Parer
Uskuf	*Üsküf*	janissary officer's cap
Vizir; Vizer	*Vezir*	vezir; vizier
Vizir Azem	*Vezir Azam*	Grand Vizier
Yagmoorlick	*Yağmurcaluk*	raincoat or cloak

Glossary

Withers' Spelling	Current Turkish Spelling	English Translation
Yoghurd	*Yoğurt*	yoghurt
Zagargee Bashaw	*Zagarcıbaşı*	Keeper of the Greyhounds; Captain of the Hounds; chief huntsman
Zebur	*Zebur*	Psalms